1

# Remember

# Reconnect

# Listen & Live

## By Karin Halliday

*First Edition 2016*

Editor: Paul Litterick

Design: Mark Fenton


ISBN: 978-0-473-36999-6


Published by Glenavary Press, Otago, NZ

## Dedication

When it comes to dedication there is never one sole person, there is always a list of people. To try and make it simple I wish to thank every single person who has helped shape my life, which has helped shape this book.

Of course none of this would have been possible without some very specific people I do need to mention:

To Rhonda who introduced me to Jay, who helped start it all off with Psychosynthesis.

To all my spiritual guides, without them I would have been lost.

To finding my soul sister Karena, bonded for many generations.

To my partner Lyndsay and daughter Aimee, I thank them for their love and support and just being there.

In memory of my brother Kevin, who died too young

# CONTENTS

## About the Author

Karin lives in New Zealand with her partner and daughter. She emigrated to NZ nineteen years ago from Scotland. She loves everything that NZ has to offer, and this is where her own healing truly began. She was an Enrolled Nurse for eight years, then a Registered Sick Children's Nurse for nineteen years. In between this she was getting rather frustrated with the Health System and became a Massage Therapist. Now she was starting to feel more connected with Health. She currently runs her own business of Body Balancing, encompassing the mind, body, spirit, believing all are connected and you can't have one without the others. Everything needs to be in balance for it to function properly. She is currently studying Chinese Medicine and Acupuncture, bringing another whole new dimension to the meaning of Health.

This is her very first book, taking four years to write. What an amazing journey in itself.

# Introduction

*We all have our own stories, we have choices.*
*These are the choices I made. This is my story*

Here I am sitting down writing my story; I ask myself, how on earth did it ever come to that? I class myself as quiet and reserved, keeping things pretty much to me and only sharing with a select few. Yet, here I am telling my story for everyone to read; pretty scary.

I have to share my story to help others, for people to see we can achieve anything we want to, and we can overcome the obstacles placed in front of us. Placed in our way as the experiences that happen to us in life, some we control, some we don't, especially as children. We have choices we can make, or not, that depends on us.

Taking a leap of faith can be liberating. When we turn around and face our fears, fear no longer has any control over us. If, however, we let fear continue to control us and stop us from what we are meant to be doing then, nothing will change and we will remain a victim.

The thought of fear makes the fear itself worse; actually facing the fear is where we get release. We have two choices as to how we live our lives: we can either fill our lives with love or we can fill them with fear. Most of us probably live in fear: fear of hurting people, fear of not getting it right, fear of being rejected, fear of what people will think or say—the list goes on and on. If we fill our lives with love, we have none of that negativity. We know we are being looked after and everything is okay. Love is the key to a happy life. But not love from another person, but rather love from yourself. We must love ourselves first, and then we can have love and give love to other people. But, a lot of the time, we fall in love and expect that person to make us happy. After a while the honeymoon period is over and we may be in a worse position than what we were before. How can we love other people if we do not love ourselves first?

Life isn't meant to be hard or unfair; it all comes down to how we look at it. When it comes to thinking that we should do it hard, we are our own worst enemies. But we have lost sight of the fact that life is meant to be enjoyed. Life is meant to be fun. Life is meant to be about having wondrous experiences and learning from them, even the ones we don't like. Our most difficult experiences are the ones we get the most learning and healing from. Difficult times are hard to take in sometimes, but when we adjust our perspective and learn not be judgmental, then we can see the learning and can start to heal. It all comes down to the choice we make: live in fear or live in love. For each situation in life there will be two different scenarios: one of fear and one of love. I often get my clients to look at the two scenarios. It's not until we can look at both and get an awareness of what each feels like and visualize how we are living in each scenario that we can get a sense there is a different way of doing things. It doesn't have to be in fear all the time. Until we can see it for ourselves we really don't believe it will change.

These are the choices I made, initially not with a lot of awareness around them. That altered as I changed and become more conscious aware. I want to share with others my own personal experience, in the hope that people who read this realise they can change their circumstances if they wish too. We no longer need to be victims to our own circumstances; we can choose to change that if we want to. That takes for all of us to literally wake up and start to become more conscious of what we do, say, think. What our belief systems are, what our self-talk is to ourselves and how we see ourselves and the world we live in. Seems big, doesn't it, but really it isn't, all of this is achievable and so much more, all it takes is for us to start being honest with ourselves, stop listening to what others say, and start listening to us!

Each and every one of us has our own answers inside of us, we just need to trust and believe that. We don't need to follow what others tell us to do, saying this is the only way. The only way for us as individuals, is to find what is right for us. It may not necessarily be right for the next person, but we are not worried about that, we are just concerned about us. Some will say that is being selfish, you are meant to put yourself last. I totally disagree with that. If we do what is right and feels right for us, then everything else falls into place very nicely and life is great. However, if we put everyone else first and ourselves last, which happens all the time, we get frustrated, things just aren't working out and our circumstances are not good. What scenario sounds best? But what does society tell us about that? Do for others first then yourself last; is that really working? For some I am sure it will be, but I think for most of us it isn't. That is where we need to be really honest with ourselves and look inside of us for our own answers.

So how did it come about I had to sit and write? I started my own inner work journey about sixteen years ago, that was consciously being aware of what I was doing. Realistically it had started long before then when I was in Britain. I just didn't realise it. One night I was sat quietly at home, in my little flat I shared with no one (it was great, my own salvation) when I was told to write. Write, why do I have to do that, what am I going to write about? Sit down and write I was told again, this time very persistently. So, being curious I did, and boy did I write. Everything you could think on came rushing out, my fingers couldn't keep up with my thoughts, and they were pouring out. From there I wrote four hundred pages about my past lives in the form of a diary and two novels. Of course, at the time I was writing, I didn't realise what they were about; I just sat down and wrote. It wasn't until about halfway through I realised just what I had written. For me, this form of writing was very therapeutic and took me to the depths of my soul as I allowed things to come to the surface. It was also something I really enjoyed; to sit down at the computer and write was a very enriching experience; it had a feeling of abandonment, release and fantasy. I could go wherever I wanted to and it didn't matter. I liked that there was no right or wrong way of doing it. I delighted in the freedom of expression. It gave me a new lease of life at a time when I really needed it.

Then in a meditation I saw an elderly gentleman sitting behind a desk, the window was open and the curtains were moving in the breeze. The room was surrounded by books. As I looked at him he reminded me of a wizard; he had long, flowing white hair and beard, and he was holding a quill in his hand for writing.

His name was Alfred, and he was one of my guides. It was through Alfred I was told to write my story; it was time.

Sounds straightforward doesn't it, write? Reading what I have just written you would think I followed that advice pretty easily. However, I didn't, I fought it all the way, I questioned it all the way; I was a sceptic, and you name it I was it. Only over time and by slowly starting to trust did that change. I could see for myself that when I followed the advice I was given it worked out, regardless of how sceptical I might have been. If I didn't follow the advice, how things worked out differently. So my perspective was starting to change, for the better.

I started writing my story four years ago, hard to believe. Initially I thought it would be a breeze, sit down, write, it will be finished in no time. Four years later isn't quite what I thought, but I had finally managed to get it finished. Then I was told to re-write what I had done. What, I said, really, yes was the answer each time. So here I am re-writing.

This is my story; this is me, the whole core and essence of me. For someone who has been very private and who has only let the odd one or two people in, this was an interesting request. How would I go opening up and sharing my story for others to read. The idea of sharing my life makes me very vulnerable and extremely open, which, again, is a new concept for me. But as I keep telling my clients, "We need to face our fears and let them go." So here I am facing my fear and sharing with all.

I need people to remember this is my story, coming from my perspective, so it will be different from others; of course it will be; they are not me. This is looking through my eyes as to all the experiences I have had in life. With what I am writing there is no blame, this is how I saw and felt it, this is about me, not about anyone else, just me. Yes others are involved and take a part, but they have their own side of events and story to tell. They are not me, they will experience it differently from me, even in the same situation; that is the way it is. So there is no blame on anyone, situation or events, this is just how it unfolded and what it has shown me, and how it has helped me grow to become the person I am today.

I am a different person today than who I was when I first came to these shores nineteen years ago. Today, I sit here as a healer and a teacher. I sit here as a person who is happy with life, who follows her guidance and intuition knowingly. I sit here as a person who is content with who I am and where I am going, but I am still clearing my issues as they come up and I get shown what I need to clear. Clearing is ongoing and does not stop until you breathe your last breath. I sit here as a person who has had many hardships and upheaval in what we call life, but each and every one of us has had to deal with hardship of some kind. I sit here as living proof we can change, and it is up to us to do the changing. Sometimes it might not seem an easy path, but it is very rich and rewarding in the fact that you find the real you. You find what you are all about and what makes you tick; not the version of you that is based on what you hear from other people or what other people tell us who we are. You find the real you, the essence of you, the soul of you. That is what happens when you embark on your inner journey. If you are brave enough to face what isn't working in your life, what needs to change and change it, you will never look back and you will wonder why you never did it sooner. The rewards far outweigh what you receive and achieve in life if you don't make the changes.

My hope and wish is that if just one person reading this book begins to make changes in their life, then my job has been achieved, because change would mean they are starting to wake up to themselves and are starting to trust and follow what they are being shown. This is no movie, this is not a rehearsal, this is our chance in life to be the person we are truly meant to be, living in peace and harmony and coming from love. Enjoy!

# Chapter One
## To be loved or not loved?

*We dance the dance together, there is no separation. We are all one*

Love is what makes the world go round, we hear all the time. All you have to do is look around at the state of the world affairs and recognize there is no love there. Of course this isn't new; it has been going on since the dawn of time really. Even back in the days of Jesus, more than 2000 years ago, everyone was fighting and there wasn't much tolerance or understanding of others. Yet Jesus taught us to trust each other and treat others how we would want to be treated. Back then we did not understand his message. It is only now we can start to get the true meaning of what he was talking about, that is so long as we don't allow other people's opinions to distort his meaning.

Yet has society changed when it comes to human behaviour? We still want to blame others when things go wrong, and we are still looking for someone to save us. So how much have we changed? We have come leaps and bounds in technology, but in human behaviour I don't think there has been much change.

He talked about keeping things simple: live simple lives, come from your heart and have no rules. Yet, we

15

have done the complete opposite. We let our mind rule us through our thoughts, but, oh how it deceives us and we are too busy to notice. We have forgotten what it is like just to stop and smell the roses. We have forgotten that time is precious and most of it we are wishing away on tomorrow, on the hope of better things. We have forgotten we live each day as it comes, for that is where we get messages to help us and where we can receive guidance if we are open to it. Alas, we keep ourselves busy and miss out on all of those messages. "Idle hands make an idle person" and "You can't just sit and not do anything" are words that ring in my ears from days of old, from our parents, and grandparents. This is what they were told and they then passed onto us, hence we have kept that cycle of being busy going. It prevents us from living in the 'Now' in the moment; once that moment has passed, we won't get it back again, yet another missed opportunity.

All of the above and much more I am guilty of doing. I have been led down that path of self-destruction and lack of self-worth, yet I had a yearning for something more and knew there was more to what we were being told. I was looking for answers, searching. It seems that for most of this lifetime I was born to search for more, for the deeper meaning of things in life. With my star sign being Scorpio, is it any wonder? Scorpios are the deep thinkers and closed books. We tend to let no one in, but when we do they are there for life; unless of course they harm us, then they had better watch out. There is nothing worse than the sting of the Scorpio tail coming out.

I love nothing more than having a great in-depth conversation about the state of affairs; what is happening for the universe, where are we going and why are we here. And yet for most of my life I have struggled with this as people like small talk and I can't do that. I like to get the nitty gritty of things and not waste time. So, during my life I have struggled in social situations. What I really wanted to talk about wasn't very interesting to most people, but it was what I loved. To help combat the feeling I didn't fit in, that there was something wrong with me, and to help get over my shyness, I would drink. And I drank a lot—in social circumstances of course! Drinking socially is an acceptable way of having fun, letting go. It is also a way of running away from life or our problems, but it's socially okay to drink, so what's the problem? Realistically, drinking is only a short term fix for a problem; eventually whatever I was trying to hide from when I drank would come and bite me in the bum.

I was born in 1965. My mother was a Catholic, my father a Protestant. When I was taken to see my father's parents they didn't want to know me because I was a Catholic. They didn't even want to look at my Christening Candle. It's hard to imagine grandparents not wanting to look at their very first grandchild, as I was to them. The hate was so embedded in them about Catholics and Protestants that they couldn't see past it, to see me as their grandchild. The way they treated me over the years never changed. They had no time for me and said I was "too much of a lady," even at four years-old! The fact is I didn't like going to visit them. Their house was messy and smelly and they cooked their food plastered in lard (fat), so yes I guess I was a "lady" because I didn't like how they did things. But they took that out on me. I always knew they didn't like me, and that used to really hurt. As a child you don't know what you have done wrong. Even though I didn't like what they did, they were still my grandparents, but not in their eyes it seemed. Then my two brothers came along, and my grandparents changed the way they treated them. My brothers were spoilt rotten. I used to watch that and it seemed unfair to me, or it was all my fault; of course it had to be, I told myself, because I must be unlovable or such a horrible person. In comes the damaging self-talk. At Christmas my mum and I would get a talc or perfume set that would be split in two, she would get one half and I would get the other. I used to laugh it off, but deep down it still hurt I didn't get my own present, while my brothers would have a present each.

It stayed like that for as long as I can remember; dad and the boys would go to his parents, while mum and I went to her parents. I used to love staying at their house, as the atmosphere was always better than at home; it felt safe. When we were in the car my brother and I would see who could spot the chimneys first and that was our sign we were getting close to our destination. We would play down on the pipeline and walk out as far as the water. When I look back at what we were allowed to do and what we allow our children to do today, it is so different. We were always outside and not allowed in until tea time. These days we don't really let our children out of our sight. While the times have certainly changed, for better or worse who knows, like anything we need to get a balance between everything we do in life. Children need to explore safely and as parents we need to let them do that and not let our own fears get in the way.

I remember I used to play with a boy at the end of the street and I had a crush on him. One day when I must have been about seven or eight he wanted to kiss me. We were standing by the lamppost and I knew he wanted to kiss me but I went running inside not knowing what to do. After I think his family moved away, but I would always look to his house wondering what he was doing and wondered what it would have been like if I had kissed him! Ah, the dramas we go through as children! Looking back they were all so innocent of course, yet they were big for me at the time.

I was brought up as a Catholic. My mum's parents were very strict Catholics and whenever we stayed at their place we had to go to Church. As a child I didn't mind. I liked to sing and look around the church, as it felt okay. As I grew up, however, that changed. I became more sceptical and started asking questions. I don't think my mum was really too bothered by it all. The only annoying thing was she made us go to Church but she never did, except when we were at her parents.' So in protest my brother and I would sit in a bus stop outside the church, even in the pouring rain, and at the end of the service we would go inside to get the Mass sheet to take home. At an early age I was starting to rebel against systems and unfairness.

I took my first Holy Communion when I was about seven years of age and Church was still exciting for me then. I still remember the two priests who were connected to my school. One was an older priest and the other young. Of course the young one was my favourite. During the Christmas of 2011 a funny thing happened when I wrote to the Church stating my intention of defecting. This decision was about cutting ties from the past I had to let go, to help me move forward. I knew, and had known for a long time, I didn't want to be a Catholic. I hadn't been in the Church for twenty odd years and I really felt a hypocrite. So in my mind it was time to do something about it. The letter I received in return was from that same young priest who had been at the Church when I was a child; I was so surprised to hear he was still there almost forty years later. It was amazing, but his letter did bring back some good memories of him.

I have good memories of the Church as a child; it was only when I was older that things changed. Perhaps it was a case of the innocence of youth compared to the cynicism of adulthood. Who knows, but I was no longer prepared to accept what the Church was saying as I didn't believe in their teachings anymore. They just didn't make sense. I soon discovered that when you ask questions you are seen as a non-believer and there was an attitude of "how dare you ask questions?" That happened a lot when I was growing up.

When I was fifteen, I refused to take my Confirmation. This was a surprise for me as I had already chosen the Saint's name I wanted to take and had learnt a lot about her. Up until that point I had been keen. I had been at a boarding school run by nuns since the age of thirteen and was there until I was sixteen. Telling Reverend Mother I wasn't doing my Confirmation did not go down well at all and I was under a lot of pressure to change my mind. I was told all the usual, "You won't go to Heaven," and "You're committing a sin." It was endless. My parents were in Germany at the time, so Reverend Mother phoned them to complain about my behaviour. She expected my parents to tell me to rethink my decision. Thankfully, my mum said there was nothing she could do to make me change my mind. That is one of the times I remember my mum sticking up for me. I also stuck to my guns and did not change my mind. From that day on, Reverend Mother never looked at me the same;

she had changed how she viewed me because I didn't take my Confirmation. Surprisingly, no one asked me why I had changed my mind. Rather, Confirmation was expected of me, regardless of what I thought or felt. All it would have taken was a bit of compassion and support to try and answer the million questions I had, yet no one did that. I was practically being ordered to my Confirmation and I couldn't.

I find it sad that we get so brainwashed into one way of thinking. Reverend Mother was unable to accept I may not believe what she did. There was no talking about it, just "Do what I say." I was fifteen and starting to get disillusioned with everything I knew about life and the world and no one could or would help me, certainly not the Church. How things had changed from loving doing my Holy Communion to being ostracized for not doing my Confirmation. Where was the empathy? Where is the understanding? Slowly, but surely, I was moving away from the Church.

Another thing I had to do at school was to go to Confession every week to confess my sins! As a teenager in a Catholic boarding school I didn't really have any; we weren't allowed to do anything. We weren't allowed to talk to boys or have makeup. We weren't really allowed music either, but most of us did. So, being forced each week to attend Confession, with nothing to confess, meant I had to make up something! I would confess things like, "I wore mascara today," or "I thought on boys." This was generally how it went as there really wasn't much else. So, tell me, what was the point? Being forced to do something does not make you believe. Instead, it has the opposite effect.

There had been times when I was feeling pretty low I had wanted to go into a Church and just sit, get some solace I guess, but I couldn't make myself walk in. Something was stopping me each time. The only time I ever did go to Church was for funerals, weddings or baptism, and every time I wanted to leave; something didn't feel right. Perhaps it was all the unsolved business I had from a teenager still looking for answers that had never been given. At this point I wouldn't have said I was angry with the Church but, as circumstances show, later on it appears I was extremely angry.

Thankfully, these days I think very differently, but I need you to remember that until 2011 I was still classed as a Catholic. What I was about to find out rocked my world as I knew it, it questioned every single thing I thought I had known, been told. Yet even in the midst of all the turmoil, anger, a sense of other knowing came through. From where I had no idea, I just knew it was there. Ultimately, what I am about to write now, was the start of my conscious decision to leave the Church.

My partner had a book called *The Secrets of the Code* by Dan Burstein. It was the unauthorised guide to the mysteries of *The Da Vinci Code*. At this point I hadn't even heard of *The Da Vinci Code* so had no idea what it would have been about. That was where I felt like I had been slapped in the face. The book gave two versions, one saying Jesus had a child with Mary Magdalene, while the other side, of course, were saying no she didn't. Whatever their belief, all the contributing authors included "facts" to prove their theories. This was the first time I had ever come across information or theories like this. Just reading this book brought up anger I had never known. I had a huge range of emotions going on, and I didn't have a clue why, or where they came from and what on earth was I going to do with it all. I felt I had been duped by the Church, that all the time they had told stories to serve themselves. Many, many mass killings had occurred all in the name of the Church. All these feelings coming up were new for me, as I always classed myself as not being an angry person! So to have these extremely strong emotions shocked me, just as much as what I was angry at. Yet amidst all the anger something felt familiar. The new stories I was reading felt more real than the stories I had been told by the Church. I had no idea if they were true or not, but they felt true to me, something I hadn't felt in a long time from the Church.

It was at this point I started to question what everything was about and try to find answers. When you start a search like this, however, it's on going and you may never find all the answers. Even then, the answers are only one person's opinion in what they write. So the best place to find your own answer is to go inside you, there you can find answers, and that was what I was starting to do. We each hold our own key, so it only through us we can find our own answers, not through anyone else. That can change things a little bit can't it? There are no leaders for us to follow except ourselves.

So here I was discovering this information for the first time and it was making sense. I kept asking how it could make sense when it went against everything I had been taught? Yet it did. For me it was like opening up a part of my brain that had been shut off for many years. That was the beginning of the end! The beginning of searching for more answers and the end of accepting what I had been told by society and the Church as true. From now on I would do my own research and work out what I believed for myself.

So then I read Dan Brown's *The Da Vinci Code* by and found it really fascinating. It was still bringing up more anger in me, but I was getting used to that by now. But when we look beyond that anger when it is gone, then you start to find the real answer and meaning. I have watched the movie two or three times now, and each time I get something else out of it. The first time I was angry at the Church, yet again, for what had occurred over history and in many ways still happening now. I was also in tears hearing about Mary Magdalene. The second time I was less angry and this time I had hope for change in salvation through the feminine, if in fact Mary Magdalene was meant to have taken over from Jesus. The third time, I had no anger, just realization that change can happen but it has to be through us being as one. For me it is about the joining of all to become one, the masculine and feminine are all one, there is no separation. I also had a lot of interest in the symbols used in ancient times and how in fact we still use today. There is so much in history we can learn from, yet it appears we are always set on repeating what happened instead of trying to learn from history.

The two books opened my closed mind, for want of a better expression, and I will always be grateful for that. This next book I am about to mention, opened me up even more, and hit a core inside me that had been hidden and forgotten about for many years. The book is called *Amma'Na'Tha* by Lesley Crossingham, which tells of Mary Magdalene and how she was named to take over the Church after Jesus, but was prevented from doing so because she was female. It also talked about her having a child, a baby girl, with Jesus. After he died she had to leave, and ended up in France.

I almost gave up reading the book, as I couldn't understand the first three chapters. Thankfully, I carried on. Well, as you can imagine, I had even more anger come up from reading this book. I had tears as well at the plight that women had to endure over centuries just for being women. I had rage at all the lies had been told over the centuries, fury at what had happened to Mary Magdalene. In amongst all this anger, I still had that feeling of familiarity. I felt I already knew the stories being told were true, but how could a book I had just read feel so true and real? This really confused me as I had no idea how this could be. Yet every ounce of my body knew it felt real. I also knew this wasn't healthy: I had to release the anger it was bringing up in me. Over time I was able to achieve that.

I sat with the ideas from *Amma'Na'Tha* for about five years, when suddenly I had the urge to read it again. I had been doing a lot of work around Mary Magdalene, who had been shown to me as one of my guides. So I read it once more; this time with a different outcome. As I hadn't understood the first three chapters, I almost didn't read them again. However, I did and boy was I glad I persevered. I totally understood the chapters this time round. In fact, part of me felt I had been there at that time. I had a sense of belonging there, a sense of knowing, yet not understanding how or why this could be. This time round I was in tears reading the book. I got so many other things from it: empathy, love, forgiveness and what life is truly all about. Gone was my anger; this time all I could feel was compassion and that life should be, and is, so simple.

We can get lost in our emotions and not find any answers when we are in them. I could have quite easily stayed in the anger that came up for me around all the books mentioned. That isn't healthy, and the only person I would be hurting is me. Anger is strong, destructive and loaded with fear. If I had stayed with this anger, particularly for the treatment of women, I would have made myself sick. Thankfully, by now I had enough understanding to know this and change it. I had to let the emotions come up by recognising and acknowledging them. Once I had done that, let them out, I could start to see what all the information presented to me was all about.

Jesus told the people and his disciples to love and treat each other as you would want to be treated. Turn your other cheek, don't use violence or anger, come from a place of love and all will be provided. Don't make up any rules, for rules will be broken and they are too hard to keep.

Simple, isn't it? Yet, do we understand that message today? Is that how we live our lives? Over time the Bible has had so many interpretations, each written by a person who has their own agenda. Interpretation of the Bible has been like Chinese Whispers: the stories have got taller and taller and more distorted in each telling of them. What do we really know today to be true or not? How can we be sure what we are being told is the truth? I always say to find the truth go with your gut instinct. If you read something and it feels right, that's what you go by, even it if underestimates and goes against everything you have been told and brought up with.

For truth to come through we must keep an open mind. Religion is very dogmatic, one sided and does not allow for questions. Jesus was all about people finding their own answers and following their own guidance, for, as He taught, each of us has the key to His kingdom, God's kingdom. It's inside of us, we just have to look. That makes more sense to me than any of the teachings I have been told over the years. Please, don't get me wrong. I'm not putting religion down. It's just that each of us has choices to make and some go for religion. That is perfectly fine. I had no choice as a child and religion was forced on me, but as an adult I did have a choice and I went for spirituality, not religion. I feed my soul every day with meditation, guidance and my intuition. That is my choice, but I ask people to keep an open mind, no matter what they follow or believe, for there are lots of questions out there that people are sometimes too scared to ask. Don't always take what you get told as Gospel, whether it is about religion or spirituality. Feel your own way. Go inside yourself and see how it sits with you. If it feels right, then that is what you go with, that is your answer. After all, our gut instinct is how spirit communicates with us, so be prepared to trust your own instinct.

The Da Vinci Code asks "would you want to destroy all faith, or would you want to renew it?" Why can't that be for all to follow what is inside them? People always seem to strive to get others to believe in what they believe in, saying this is the only way. Should it really be like that? Why can't we accept that whatever people believe in is okay, even if it is different from what you believe in? Why do we all have to believe in the same thing or way? We are all individuals and think different so it is obvious we are going to believe in dissimilar things. Why have other opinions forced on us? Why can't we find out for ourselves what we believe and others accept that? So surely to renew faith would be for each of us to look inside us and find out what we as individuals believe in. Imagine what that could do for humankind.

After finishing this chapter I took our dog for a walk and had a laugh to myself at what I had written. Nothing like leaping straight in the deep end by talking about religion! When I was writing up my notes for the book, religion was the first thing I started to write about too, so I guess that is the way it is meant to be. Now you can see why I don't do small talk!

# CHAPTER TWO
## Lots of travel

*Trust in the unseen, trust in the unknown and follow
your heart always.*

My dad was in the British Army, so we travelled a lot.
But we were lucky when it came to moving around with
the Army, as dad was based in Edinburgh for seven years
when I was younger, so I was able to do most of my
primary schooling in one place. We moved from
Germany to Edinburgh when I was four. Edinburgh was
the place I called home, until I came to New Zealand. I
would often get asked where my home was and I
struggled to answer as we never stayed in one place long
enough for me to feel connected. So, I called Edinburgh
home because we stayed there the longest and it stayed
that way. I can remember some things from our time
there, like the park, our flat and the shops. I remember
there was a huge hill I quite often had to use to get to the
shops. It was not fun having to climb it! I always
remember having to get the public bus to go to school.
Once at the bus stop there was a man having a seizure
and everyone was just standing around looking at him,
not doing anything, just staring. I remember thinking,
"That's not fair, someone should be helping him, not
staring." This memory always came back to me when I
was looking after a patient who was an epileptic. I felt

quite deeply for that man in the bus stop no one was helping.

New entrant class, ah doesn't that take you back! One of the few things I remember from that time was the teacher. She seemed to me very old (I guess anyone seems old to a young person) and she was very strict. Mum told me once about what happened with this teacher when she went to a parents evening with her sister. The teacher claimed she had never been more frustrated with a child as she was with me. She went on to tell mum and my aunt she had told the class to draw a horse. I had replied, "No! I want to draw a house." "No," the teacher said, "you will draw a horse." "No," I said, "I will draw a house." and I drew a house as I really didn't want to draw a horse. The teacher obviously didn't like my attitude and told the story to my mum and aunt with great gusto. I, of course, thought it quite funny when I was told the story.

Now my own daughter is at school she keeps asking for stories of the things I did when I was younger. I told her this story and she thinks it's great, of course. I have to tell it over and over again. The only problem with this is I hope she doesn't decide to do something similar! I wouldn't be able to have much come back on it, would I: "Well, you said that's what you did when you were younger, so why can't I?" And of course this would be very true, but thankfully it's quite different today at school.

It's funny how all these memories of not nice teachers come to mind when I enter into a school. It makes me feel like I am a child again, not an adult! Trying to choose which school my daughter should go to was a challenge, as I kept saying, "Well when I was at school…" The school we chose for her is very liberal and forward thinking. I feel that comes from the Principal down: happy staff, happy children, and happy school. Why couldn't it have been like that in my day, I ask? Of course, it was very different thinking back then.

When I first started school I remember hiding under the coats in the cloakroom at playtime and lunchtime as I didn't want to go outside. I don't think I knew what to do or I didn't feel safe. I'm not entirely sure. Years later I revisited my inner child and sat with her under those coats and I saw she was absolutely petrified of playing and having fun. It took a long time to coax her out, but she did eventually. My inner child grew up too fast because of what happened to her and she never trusted many people. That was carried on into adult life and it wasn't until I started therapy that it all became clear as to why. So having fun wasn't an option for her when she started school; it seemed all quite foreign to her.

I do remember I was much better playing with just one person rather than having a few friends around. The funny thing is, it's still like that today. I may not have lots of friends but the ones I do have are very special and dear to me. Others may prefer having lots of friends around but I don't and, looking back, I never have. I am much better in a one to one situation. It has taken a lot of years to say that but now I know I am actually okay with it, that's who I am. Many times as I was growing up I would question why I was not like other people, why I couldn't talk a lot. I would always ask, "why, why, why?" Now, as an adult, I understand, but as a child I struggled.

I don't remember in great detail the rest of my days in primary school. I only remember two teachers, well three including my New Entrant teacher. One teacher I remember for her gorgeous long straight hair and the fact she was very pretty. The other was my maths teacher and I really liked him as he encouraged me in my maths and convinced me I could do it. "Wow!" I thought, "I can do maths." When I went to boarding school, however, I didn't do quite so well at maths because of the teacher and her lack of influence and encouragement. She was younger than some of the other teachers we had. So, initially, we thought, "Great! This will be good, someone young." Well, that didn't last too long as every time she walked into the classroom she would shout, and I mean shout, "STAND!" and of course we had to stand on her command when she entered the room. This didn't go down too well and I of course was one of the rebellious one who refused to comply. I would get up **very** slowly and continue standing until the others were already sitting down again. Needless to say, my maths went down the gurgler after that as I lost interest pretty rapidly and she never offered encouragement. This was quite sad as I did enjoy maths. Going from a teacher who encouraged a great deal, to another who demanded respect and never got it was demoralizing. Oh, it amazes me how much influence a teacher can have on a child, and I am sure there are lots and lots of very similar stories out there.

I went from Edinburgh to England for two years and continued my schooling there. The only thing I remember from this time was when we went swimming with the school. The teacher ordered all those who could swim into the deep end. I, of course, thought I could swim. I was about to find out however, the reality was very different. I jumped in with huge enthusiasm, only to quickly discover I was struggling to keep afloat. The teacher had to jump in with glasses and all on to save me. Well, I have never been so affronted in my whole life. Word had even spread around the school before I got back; how, I have no idea, as this was prior to mobile phones, but it did. After that incident I was scared to go into the pool. Later in life I got over my fear by jumping in the deep end and I managed to swim to the other end this time. It was very uneventful!

Then my dad was posted to Germany so it was agreed I would go to boarding school. The choice was mine. At the time I hated both my parents. I know hate is a strong word but, at the age of twelve or thirteen, I did hate my parents. I always used to wish they would get divorced as they were always arguing and fighting, which was not nice. Later on, when I was about eighteen, and dad left for the first time, I told my mum this. So boarding school it was, and what's more it was a convent in South England. It was chosen mainly so I could stay with my aunt at the weekend. That worked well for about a year, but then it became the worse of two evils: to stay at school or go to my aunt's place. She had no children of her own and everything I did was not good enough, whether it was using spray deodorant, having shoes with a small heel, using mascara; this list went on, she always managed to find something to criticize. In the end I believed I was better off at school, so I stayed there for the weekends.

My greatest teacher at boarding school was the history teacher. Every lesson we would digress and end up talking about something else. I loved it! She was open to different ideas and she had a great amount of knowledge she was willing to share with the bunch of lost souls who were the students in her class. My year level was known as the rebels, which didn't go down too well. Even our graduation into Sixth Form never happened as we were deemed not to be worthy! So we became Upper Fifth instead! It was quite funny.

When we were getting close to doing our exams we committed the ultimate act of rebellion by refusing to study or even sit our exams! Imagine that, saying "No!" to the nuns. It was not a good look. So two weeks before the exams some monks were brought in to talk to us. That day was the saving of us and our exams. I can remember sitting down with a monk and thinking, "I'm not changing my mind. They can't make us do anything." Afterwards, I felt so different. In fact the whole class did and it was amazing. To this day I still can't really remember what happened that day or what they said to us. All I do know is that we all buckled down and two weeks later sat our exams and passed! I think the monks said we were hurting ourselves, no one else. We also talked a bit about the nuns, but again can't actually remember what was said! I do know there was a huge presence that day with the monks around. I have never really thought about it much until recently. It felt different when they were there; maybe it was because they were treating us like adults and it felt we were being listened to, or maybe there was a higher purpose with their presence; who knows?

Normally the leaving class would be presented with a gift at the end of the year in recognition of all their achievements. However, our class received nothing! Again, it didn't really bother us too much, but it was a little sad they couldn't see past what they believed was bad behaviour in the fact we had dared defy them. Well, over the years I have learnt there is always more to a person than how they behave. There is usually a reason behind a person's behaviour, but the nuns never bothered to see that. All they could see was that, by not doing as we were told, we were not setting a good example for the other children. As mentioned previously, it was at this time I refused to do my Confirmation. This decision was yet another nail added to my coffin in the nuns' eyes. A couple of years later, I heard the school had closed down; not quite up to standards! I laughed at that thinking we could have told you that a few years ago!

After battling as a child to travel to new places, being shy, being nervous when starting at a new school and taking a while to make friends, I thought life would be easier as an adult. However, I found I couldn't settle, so I continued the cycle of moving around. I stayed in Edinburgh when I first qualified as an Enrolled Nurse, then I joined the Royal Air force for four years, going to England and Germany. After I moved back to Edinburgh, then Dumfries, Hull and onto the big smoke of London, where I stayed for four-five years, but managed to move residences a few times in that short period. Then it was back to Edinburgh to 'settle,' but I couldn't commit to Edinburgh long term as nothing had changed. I left after about nine months and headed back to London as a stop gap until I got everything ready to go to over to New Zealand. In between all this I have been to many places on holiday. One of them was America, specifically to go to Graceland and Disneyland. I always wanted to go as a child but it never happened, so as an adult I made sure I did go; absolutely amazing.

Before choosing to come to New Zealand I had the chance to work in Africa with VSO to teach nursing in one of the schools there. I was all set to go, but something was niggling me not to. Then the chance to travel to New Zealand came up and I had to choose between the two. I chose New Zealand. Looking back I can now see why I wasn't ready to go to Africa. I had my own inner demons to deal with at that time. As life unfolds and I look back, I can now see why I made this choice. Africa was not the right place for me to do this. At the time, however, I didn't understand this but I trusted my intuition; which is something I have always done but never realised I was doing it, if that makes sense.

Travel has been my friend and foe. When younger I had no choice with regard to travel. As an Army family we had to move: foe; as an adult I chose to travel: friend. On a serious note, with travel I have always been looking for somewhere else to go, always thinking what's on the other side. That saying, "the grass is greener on the other side," is very true. Most of my life has been spent searching and looking but I had no idea what for. I could never settle and worried I might miss out on something because I stayed in one place. So when the urge took me, I went. Everyone kept asking, "when are you going to settle down," and "when are you going to buy a house?" "When, when…" all the time. I also was asked if I was happy travelling and moving all the time. For some of the time I was, as moving to a new place was how I got my buzz then; when it got boring or what I perceived as boring, I moved again. So yes, I enjoyed it and have absolutely no regrets, but something was missing; that much I knew, I just didn't know what. When I was growing up I always said I wasn't going to get married until I had seen the world. I never wanted to buy my own place either, as that would tie me down too much and I didn't want that responsibility. I wanted to have the freedom of doing what I wanted, when I wanted. So I always rented, shared places with others or, towards the end of my single days, lived by myself and created my own little haven.

It seemed I was going to keep up the same tradition when I moved to New Zealand. I lived in Auckland for about ten months before moving to Queenstown in the South Island. Everyone at work thought I was mad moving to the South Island. In Queenstown there wasn't enough work so I had to leave after a few months. I filled the car to leave which left me with five dollars in my pocket, literally, until I got a job working in the Paediatric unit. I stayed in Dunedin for five years, then up to Central Otago for eighteen months then over to Australia for two years then finally back to Central Otago and have been here now for nine years. Does this mean I am finally settled; who knows? What I have found that once Central Otago gets in your blood that's it, there is no escaping it: surrounded by hills and with the Alps not far away, it is one of the driest places to live in New Zealand and it certainly has a unique feel about it.

I have been in New Zealand now for nineteen years and fully intend to stay here. Apparently, and unbeknown to me at the time, my friends in Scotland had given me six months. They felt if I wasn't back within that time I would probably stay! They were right. New Zealand is now home and it felt that way from the moment I set foot on these shores, albeit it for a holiday initially.

So I have travelled and lived in many houses and had countless nursing jobs. The longest I ever stayed in one place was about eighteen months to two years, and then I would get bored and move on. When I was in Dunedin I actually broke quite a few of those cycles, and stayed in one job for three years, never heard of before, and I had remained in the same city for five years, again another record broken. Finally I could see I was starting to stop the cycles I once used to do. Yeah things were beginning to change; I was changing, more importantly.

## Chapter Three
## How it all began

*Believe in yourself; believe in your dreams,*
*for they can come true*

Dunedin was where it all really changed. As I have said to my clients many a time, if we don't make the changes we need ourselves, then we are forced to make them. That can be through a crisis or hitting a brick wall. When I talk to my clients it is mainly through experiences I went through. When you are in the business of helping others, you can't help anyone until you have helped yourself first. That is the golden rule of healing. We must heal ourselves first, otherwise it is pointless. We can't take anyone where we haven't been ourselves.

So I had my hand forced to change when I fractured my neck! That was a huge wake up call, and even then it still took a while for it to really sink in. Ever since I can remember I have been around alcohol. I probably had my first taste of it when I was fifteen. We were at home in Germany at the time and mum said she would prefer we tried alcohol at home rather than outside, she could keep an eye on us. I had drunk Martini, and was sick for quite a while afterwards. I swore off alcohol then, and I have never touched Martini since; the smell puts me off straight away.

Everything I have chosen to do has always been sociable and with alcohol: nursing, the Air Force, living a few houses down from our local pub in London: that was great as we used to get locked in! Good times, but alcohol was always involved. My dad was a heavy drinker, almost bordering on alcoholism I would say. There were many times on a Friday after work he would get in his car and drive; he couldn't stand, let alone drive, yet he did. How on earth he ever managed to get home is beyond me. I used to dread every Friday because of his drinking, for years. So then it came to my turn. After witnessing what alcohol had done to my dad I really didn't think I would get into the drinking scene, but I did.

Alcohol was my friend for many years, as it helped me over my shyness. It's great for that, as you lose all inhibitions and can do crazy things, all in the name of being drunk! The stories I could write about everything that happened through alcohol would take another book itself, but that's not what this book is about.

Following many years of drinking, alcohol starts to take its toll on you. After a while it stops becoming fun anymore. It no longer lifts you up but takes you down. There starts the spiral that ends with hitting rock bottom. You are unhappy when you drink, yet you are just as unhappy when you don't drink. I had known this for a few years before I was forced to stop. I was drinking now to hide from something, but I didn't know what. I was drinking to hide from pain I had, but I didn't know why. I was drinking because I was extremely unhappy. What I call my picker-upper was no longer working. Each time I had a drink I was sinking further and further down, probably into depression, but for a long time I refused to see that. I was depressed, using alcohol to hide it, to fill that gaping hole in the pit of my stomach. Denial was the name of the game. I'm not depressed, I have a job, I have friends, I have my life together, or so I thought! But was I happy, what is happiness? I felt happy when drinking, then when I stopped being happy it changed.

The fateful night at Christmas when I had one too many orange juices! And what was it all over, a man! I had this huge crush on a work colleague and I thought I was very clever in the fact he didn't know. Wrong, I found out that night he had known all along. I was mortified, embarrassed, to name two of the horrible feelings I had about myself. So I got drunk, no, I got plastered is the only way to describe it. We were all on the dance floor and I just fell backwards for no reason, straight onto hard flooring: bang number One. Then, a little bit later, I did the exact same again: bang number Two. This time a friend put me in a taxi to take me home. The next day, boy did I suffer; I had concussion for two days. I was in denial that it was concussion, as that meant it was more serious than I was willing to admit to myself.

I went back to work and we all laughed, of course, about what had happened. If nothing else I was used to people laughing at the craziness of what I used to do. I was okay with that. On New Year's Eve, not a drop of alcohol had passed my lips I may add! We went to the beach to watch the sunset as it was the start of the millennium and wanted to do something different, it was great. In the car coming back I turned around and couldn't move, my neck had given way. I was working that afternoon and of course everyone had thought I had been drinking, but I hadn't. Eventually I was convinced to go for an x-ray; which I did, bearing in mind this is a week later after my fall. They asked me in the x-ray department have I had any falls recently; no I said, forgetting about the week before or still being in denial about it all. There it was in black and white a small fracture off my C6, there was a small chip of the bone floating around in my neck, yikes!

Shock, disbelief and numerous other ways to describe how I felt all came flooding in. But again I was still in denial; this isn't too serious I was saying to myself. Even though I was in a neck collar and given strong pain relief, still not bad I said! It wasn't until I took the x-ray back and showed one of our doctors I guess the seriousness of it all was starting to kick in. No one was laughing this time, least of all me.

When this happened I was living by myself which I loved, as my days of having flatmates were over. I would think nothing of having a bottle of wine a night by myself. Each night going home I would get a bottle, and I knew it was more habit than anything, but how do you break a habit? I broke that habit when I broke my neck! A hard lesson to learn, you bet it was. I still wasn't out of the woods yet though. About a month later we went to a party and I had one drink, just one! I was still feeling the effects of previous events. On the way out the paving was really unsteady and I fell! Landing on my face, I couldn't believe it, I had fallen again and this time with only having had one drink. Of course everyone thought I had been drinking more than one but I hadn't. The lesson I was learning was getting harder as I was a stubborn student, one still very much in denial.

I never touched a drop of alcohol for a long time after that. Even to this day I have never been drunk again. I was petrified of drinking and getting to that stage of drunkenness. It wasn't an easy road giving up alcohol, as everyone sees you as a fun person when you are drinking, but when you stop you're not so funny anymore. Everyone else around you is drunk and you are sober, that takes a lot to get used to. About six weeks after breaking my neck I had a friend's wedding to go to in the North Island. I knew I shouldn't go as I knew in myself I wasn't in a good place. I went against my own intuition, which hasn't been the first time, and it was a disaster. Right from the start I knew I shouldn't be there but I was only there because it was a very good friend and I didn't want to let her down. I not only let her down that night but also myself. I said then I would follow more of my own intuition rather than doing what I think I should do for other people. There were still a few more lessons to learn in that before I finally got the lesson.

I was starting to get addicted to the painkillers I had been given: they were strong. Each time I tried to go without one I couldn't do it. So I took drastic action as I realised that if I didn't stop taking them now I wouldn't be able to stop. So I went cold turkey one night and stopped. Well for the next twenty four hours I was having flashbacks, and going to places I had no idea where they were. I was wide awake it felt for the whole twenty-four hours, these tablets were scary. After I was fine, but it was pretty close to becoming addicted to them though. I had been on them for a month when I came off them. The painkillers I had been given were Tramadol.

Another time I went cold turkey and stopped drinking coffee. Again it used to lift me up, but like the alcohol it was having the opposite effect. I went from having six to seven cups of strong coffee a day to none. It took about a week for the caffeine to get out of my system. The first three days were horrendous: headaches, sleepiness, irritability: you name it I had it. But I stuck with it as I knew I would come alright at the end. On the fourth day things started to change as I was coming back up. By the seventh day the caffeine was out of my system and I have never touched a coffee again. I still like the smell of it I just don't want to drink it anymore and haven't. My work colleagues would always ask how many coffees I had taken when they came on for work in the afternoon, as I guess I was sometimes quite hyper! After six or seven that would do it to you.

Alcohol was what I used to try and help me feel better, but it wasn't working as I had been clearly shown. I guess some people would use anti-depressants, I used alcohol. Either way they work for a short while but until we get to the cause of what is happening we are only masking the symptoms and not getting to the root of it all. When I work on someone's body I quite often say that where they have the complaint, where it is sore, that's just the symptom; the cause is coming from elsewhere and that is what we need to access. As always there is more to the problem as first thought. So we can use all the tricks of the trade to fool ourselves we feel fine, nothing wrong with me, yet we sink deeper and deeper into the hole until the only way out is to finally turn around and look within ourselves. Start to be honest with ourselves and to heal. That takes courage and seems a long hard road, but honestly it isn't. It is the most rewarding road you will ever embark on, as it is your inner journey that will take you to the real you. Will the real person stand up please, and you will with your head held high for you will know the real you. Not the one that is in denial, like I was. I was desperately lonely and trying to find someone to love me, by using alcohol. Doesn't work in the end it only brings more heartache. Finally you get to stand on your own two feet and say look at what I have achieved all by myself. Well not quite by yourself, for when we embark on the inner journey we have many guides, angels and helpers, so we are never actually alone. We never do this work by ourselves, there is always help, all we have to do is ask and we shall receive.

I have had many great nights out, had wonderful laughs, great times, laughed hard, fooled around a lot, and cried a lot with alcohol. It has been a good friend for many years. I still savour all those good times I had when using it. But like anything there comes a time when the behaviour is no longer working, it needs to stop. If it is becoming destructive and destroying your life slowly then it has to stop. What are we running or hiding from? Whether it is alcohol, drugs, cigarettes, sex, gambling they are all addictive behaviours. We all use them at some stage in our life, but stop and take a closer look to see why you are using them. You may be surprised, it may possibly seem scary too, but when we add a bit of light to a problem how that changes everything when we start to see clearly. It takes strength and courage and every single person has that ability in them, it's just we have never been told. Everyone has the key to unlock the inner door, deep inside of them. Take that step forward, take the plunge into the unknown and you will never look back; you will only go forward with confidence. I once read a book that had an amazing saying in it, it said, "*the first child*

*born of doubt is of fear, the first child born of courage is of love"*
(sadly I can't remember what book; I have read so many).

Everything happens for a reason, just at the time it is hard to see how and why, but it does. After I fractured my neck I started to see a chiropractor, I had no idea what they were all about but it was recommended to me so I went. After a few sessions he turned around to me and said we will be having a relationship for about the next twenty years, my body was that bad it would always need fixing and adjusting! It's just as well I trusted this man, for I did, my body was in his hands so to speak, and he was a good teacher. Certainly in the beginning my body needed a lot of work, but the more inner work I done on myself that shifted and cleared away a lot.

Then having a massage was recommend to me; I had no real idea what that was about either. But again I trusted and looked up the Yellow Pages and this one name kept jumping out at me. I rang and made an appointment. I will always remember my very first visit; I was petrified. Even more so when she said take your clothes off! What, "why do I have to take my clothes off?" That was how naïve I was at the time! Hard to believe massage is now my line of work when you see how it started off for me! Life does change. I don't think I moved the whole entire hour I was on the table, relax I certainly did not. My neck was as stiff as a board, of course it was after the injury I had. When she was working on my body I kept thinking, "what is she doing, where are her hands going, the whole time?" Now I look back and laugh at this and will quite often share this story with clients, particularly if some look scared or it is their first time. But something was working as I kept going back. In fact I couldn't wait to get there, get the clothes off and on that table to relax, it was great.

We became good friends for a while and had amazing chats about the meaning of life and spiritual things; well actually she would talk about a lot and I would listen as all of this was new to me. Intrigued I was, so when she mentioned Psychosynthesis where you journey inside of you by sitting or lying down, with your eyes closed. The best way to describe it at this stage is a bit like hypnotherapy. You go to a different place, a different space; you follow what your heart tells you to do and not your mind. This is how you can find the inner you.

Great, I thought, that sounds like me. I had done some counselling when I lived in London. Even back then I knew something wasn't right I just didn't know what. So I plucked up the courage to see a counsellor. I remember the first day I was heading to see him, I got pretty scared thinking, "I don't need to go, I haven't got anything to talk about; I can buy a new top for the price of the sessions I am going to pay." All these thoughts were running through my head to try and stop me from going. Somehow I got myself on the tube and went. The roof of my mouth was parched, scared, you bet I was. What was I going to say, I had nothing to say to him, what if I get there and nothing gets said for the hour and half. My stomach was going ten to the dozen, as it normally does when I'm nervous. I can remember the clock ticking away in the hall while I was waiting for him to finish with his previous client. I kept thinking I could make a quick exit out of the door before he comes out. It was like my bottom was glued to the seat and I wasn't allowed to move! Too late, I had to go in; it had to be the quickest hour and half I had ever known in my life. Talk; I never stopped!

I kept going for a year and half and boy did it open up a can of worms. I never realised I had so much inside hidden, shoved down, and not dealt with. I was angry at everyone and everything just about. They done this to me, that's their fault I'm like this, and on it went. I wasn't told how to cope with that anger or what to do with it, it came up and I was expected to deal with it, but how? So I stayed angry. No one told me to go and scream from the top of my voice, no one told me ways of how to release anger. Looking back I was probably like a ticking time bomb waiting to explode. The counselling was good, absolutely, but I had emotions I had no idea what to do with, so they stayed inside of me festering away.

So when I heard about Psychosynthesis I really thought that sounds like a cool place where you go to, you don't have to delve into things too much! I may have regretted thinking that on my very first session. It was different alright, I sat down, and not as nervous as I was when I went for my first counselling session in London. I thought I had an understanding of what I was about to embark on! So I met Jay for the first time, little English lady, I had a chuckle at that with me being Scottish, the battle of the two ancient foes. We chatted for a few moments, she told me to close my eyes and take some deep breaths, great, I'm thinking, this is where I can go to la-la land. Then she said, now tell me how you feel! Well, you could have bolted me on the head with a hammer and I still wouldn't have moved. I froze with fear: feel, tell you how I feel, I can't do this, I have no idea about how I feel, I don't know. This isn't for me after all, get me out of here. Move, no, I was rock solid stuck in my chair, my buttocks were going nowhere. Get me out of here I'm screaming in my head. So of course when she asked me how I felt, there was silence from my end, nothing for a few moments. Somehow words were coming out of my mouth, I have no idea how, the words were coming out but I was still sat rigid.

I had private sessions for about a year with Jay, things were shifting inside of me, and then I started the course which took me in even deeper. How I describe the process to people is how it was as described to me. It's like an onion, you take a layer off at a time, and go down and down until you get to the main core issue you may have. So you go down gradually as the body would not cope if the process was too fast, you would go into shock and not be able to clear anything at all. That of course is defeating the object. The main reason you do this work is to get to know the real you, get away from all ideas you have about yourself that people have said to you over your lifetime. This is about you, finding your connection with the universe or God depends on what you believe in. At that time the universe worked very well for me, I wasn't able to mention the word God. If that name had been mentioned I think I would have bolted out the door there and then. The universe really does know how to look out for us and it really does have our interest at heart. It wants us to succeed and become who we are in this lifetime.

That was my introduction into Psychosynthesis which became a huge part of my life, as did Jay and still is. She is still a good mentor and friend to this day.

For those who don't know Dunedin it gets called the Edinburgh of the south. You walk down the main street and it's called George Street, then you come across Princess Street, then you have Hanover Street, all of these Streets are in Edinburgh. Needless to say I felt very much at home there. They were however missing one of the important streets of all called Rose Street, for back in Edinburgh that is the main street that has all the pubs in it. You can't walk from one end to the other going in all of them and remembering you have done it, it's virtually impossible. So here I was on the other side of the world being in the Edinburgh of the south, what are the odds!

# Chapter Four
## Psychosynthesis, change is happening

*There is a bigger plan, we are all part of that plan; we just need to remember, remember where we come from*

Whenever I do things if I have a sense of what I think it is about it generally turns out to be the opposite. Realistically if I knew half the time what I was letting myself in for I wouldn't go there, not even a little. So isn't it just as well I don't really know! How many of us say today I am going to look at all my inner rubbish; as a rule we don't. Yet that is what we should be doing. None of this work I have done came easy; I fought it all the way. I asked, questioned and doubted which I think is being healthy. As long as I adjust with it and not let anything like fear stop that change from happening.

As mentioned earlier, I don't do well with big numbers of people; I like one to one or small groups. I clam up and feel threatened when in big groups. So when Jay spoke to me about doing the course I thought that sounds good. I asked how many people. Not many, she said she thought about five to seven depending on the people. It was bordering on a lot for me but I thought I can handle that. Then just before the course started I asked how many, ten she said. Ten I shouted really, you said it was only going to be a few, well that's the funny thing, she said, everyone is meant to be doing it, so ten it is. I was now starting to have second thoughts about the course because of the number. Still, somehow, I didn't pull out and went along.

There were seven women and three men. I really struggled especially when I saw the men. I wouldn't be able to talk with men around, I thought, I was so used to it always being women. Thankfully the group that we had everyone was an amazing person in their own right. Everyone had issues but we all had a common goal to help ourselves. The group was great and I loved everyone in it. It wasn't easy at the beginning though it was only through time it got better. That is the beauty of doing a course on your inner self; you deal with all your hang ups and find just where they come from and deal with them. Don't get me wrong; this wasn't a plain sailing course, it was tough no doubt there, but the rewards far outweighed the hard times. When you can see how much you are changing in yourself, it compels you to work more. You have skills and tools you have been given, that you use in your everyday life to help you. No longer will you be the person you once were; you are a truer version of yourself that has been hidden; now they are allowed to come out and shine. When you see and feel that within yourself, there is never a greater feeling. Now you are starting to reap the rewards of your hard work.

I will always remember one of the sessions we had on the course. We were told to go to our heart space and tell each other person in the group what we thought of them. If I thought the course had pushed my buttons up until now; boy was I wrong. This pushed them all big time. I was fuming, angry and ropeable all at once. However, none of these words really describe what I felt as the feeling was so strong and something I had never experienced (or admitted to) before and I was very uncomfortable. I glared at Jay with, "What are you doing to me?" thoughts racing through my head. I kept looking at the door behind me, trying to will myself to get up out of my chair and move, but I couldn't move, I just couldn't ( how many times has that happened before!). There was no avoiding it, I am going to have to be honest with everyone. As things got started I didn't talk to the two girls on either side of me, I was still too angry. I realise now that really I was scared of what other people would say about me. All of my life I had overheard people talk about me and their words were never nice, so I automatically assumed that was going to be the case again. However, I was astonished at what everyone said about me as their words were so positive.

Then it came to my turn. I stood up and was shaking like a leaf, I took a few deep breaths and started to speak. "Well this is okay," I thought. I wasn't saying anything nasty, I was just speaking from the heart, and surprisingly it felt okay. Then I spoke to Jay and even that was okay. Wow! I had just spoken the truth in a healthy, non-violent way. My words had come directly from my heart and it felt good. But this was different from my other experiences in life as we were talking from our hearts not from our head; and in our hearts is only love. Coming from love meant it was okay, it was safe. Then Jay told me I was a shaman and that we would be friends for a very long time. I was blown away by that.

Afterwards I told the others how angry and mad I was at the start of the session. I was surprised when everyone said they could see that. The two girls who had been sitting next to me said they could actually feel my mood;

and I had been thinking I had successfully hidden my feelings, how wrong I was.

The whole experience felt very invigorating and empowering. I learnt it is okay to speak the truth, especially when you come from your heart. When you are in that space nothing matters because all you feel is love and compassion. If you have never felt that purity in the heart space before, it is truly amazing when you do feel it for the first time.

Before I knew it the year was up and I was left wondering where the time had gone. I had survived a year and, more importantly, I wanted to go ahead and do the second year of the course. Jay told us to go away and write about why we should do the next year. As our homework each week was to delve into ourselves through writing and meditating and just being, it was no surprise we had to write to see if we were to carry on. As always, I thought I had the answer, so imagine my surprise, when, in my writing and meditation, I was told, "No!" Each time I wrote I got the same answer. I really struggled with it as I wanted to be a therapist and believed that another year with Jay would help me to realise my dream. I couldn't understand why was I getting told no, and of course I questioned why I was writing "No" all the time. I even wondered if I was fighting the process. I had trusted everything I had written during the whole year, so I was confused as to why I could not trust my writing now. So, in the end, I accepted I had to go with it. I had believed I was going to become a therapist, but it seemed those plans had been blown out of the water. I guess I shouldn't have been surprised by this change of plans, as whenever I thought I knew what I was going to do in life, things usually turned out to be the opposite.

It just goes to show there is a bigger plan, but there are times when we can't see it. It took eleven years for me to understand why and get closure on being guided away from continuing the course with Jay, especially when I had been convinced I was meant to do it. Eleven years later I was given a second chance to take the second year of the course, "Yes," I thought, "here we go. Now I can become a therapist. Now I am ready. Now is the time for me to do it," were the thoughts going through my head. It still sat with me I was to become a counsellor. In my mind the only way to achieve this was through Psychosynthesis, not mainstream counselling. I wanted to be a spiritual counsellor who encompassed everything: body, mind and soul, all joined together, not separate. So, here I was, believing I would finally get to do it after all these years. I was excited.

I sat down to do my meditation and to seek guidance about the course, and you guessed it, again I was told, "No!" Initially I kept going back and asking, "Are you sure?" The answer was always a definite "Yes!" It was clear I was not meant to do the course. This time however, being a little wiser and more in tune with myself, I clearly saw and heard why the course was not for me. I was told I was a healer and a teacher and I was already doing what I was meant to be. I help people, and, yes, sometimes I do a bit of counselling with my clients anyway, so you see, without realizing it, I was already doing exactly what I wanted, it just wasn't under the name counsellor. Eleven years later I understood I was to help people learn about and understand the energies of the human body and universe and how we are all connected to the land and universe. I work with bodies; I help people understand a bit more about their own bodies. Now I could understand why I was told "No" eleven years ago. Now I could see there was a bigger picture, so I finally let my longing to do the course go as I no longer doubted what I was told. Rather, I trusted and believed, and was happy to follow what we call the process of life. Life really is quite amazing and teaches us so much if we are willing to take the time and listen to what we get told from our intuition, our inner knowing.

I was now starting to be consciously aware of my spiritual journey and I could feel myself waking up; after all, we are spiritual beings. I once read, *"We are spiritual beings in a physical body,"* which I think is very fitting. Many of us have forgotten this as we have been fixated on the physical aspect of life, work and home. We have forgotten we are here to learn and grow, to remember who we truly are, where we have come from. Our emotions are our guides as to how we are feeling. Yes, we are meant to feel our emotions, but not be led by them; for it is then we get led astray and start to identify with them. Our emotions are meant to help show us when something isn't right inside of us. Yet, when we feel bad we look to blame others for the feeling, instead of going inside of us.

We are human and as human we have unique experiences which cause emotional responses in us. It is important to remember, however, that our overall being is of spirit, we come from there and we will go back there—wherever that is. Some say we are born of the stars and will go back to the stars. Ultimately, we will go back to "that place," be it the stars, Heaven or someplace similar; it all depends on what we have been brought up on to believe, what our beliefs systems are.

It's our belief system, what we have been brought up to believe, that can stop us from growing and learning as our beliefs can mean we are not open to other ways of thinking. So we need to keep an open mind and be open to new possibilities. Let's face it, most of us believe in what we get told at school. But I wonder if what we learnt at school is the only way of doing things. Perhaps there are other possibilities and one size does not necessarily fit all.

That was what the Psychosynthesis course assisted me with. It helped me start to recognize what my belief patterns were. I was encouraged and supported to go deep down inside myself and see what was damaging and what wasn't. I was able to eliminate those beliefs that were controlling and leading me astray. I was now competent enough to let other belief patterns come to the surface, and recognize they were there to help me, not control or sabotage me. I realised most belief patterns don't work anymore as most have been instilled by fear and it's the fear that holds us back, keeps us prisoner in our own bodies and minds. This, I realised, was the difference between the counselling sessions when I lived in London and Psychosynthesis. The latter takes you down into your heart, your inner self. It acknowledges everything about you and you learn to let go of those beliefs, emotions or anything holding you back. When you do this you start to change as a person for the better. By letting go you are saying fear is no longer a part of your world and your mind will no longer hold you prisoner. The counselling brought up emotions, but there was no way of releasing them. The difference with counselling is you come from your mind, and it's your mind that wants to rule you and stops you from changing because, when you do change, your mind no longer has any control over you, and that scares the mind. It will do anything to prevent you from doing this. It will tell you anything to impede you. It will run amuck with your thoughts in an attempt to stop you; to keep control the mind operates from fear. As I mentioned before it is only the thought of fear makes fear worse. Facing your fears is nothing compared to what your mind tells you about that fear! Please bear in mind there is nothing wrong with normal counselling; it was through doing counselling that a door started to open up for me. But we need to probe deeper than perhaps counselling allows. To find the answers we need to go inside to discover them, for we each hold the answers inside of us.

As doors continued to open, I went further on my spiritual journey and investigated other ways of being. I wanted to know what else was out there and what other teachings there were. Now there was no stopping me. After Psychosynthesis I went to Siddha Yoga, which was great. There were lots of meditations and I learnt about new Gurus from India from reading their teachings and listening to what they were saying. But I was there for a short while, took what I needed, and moved onto the next experience. At this point in time I kept asking, "Why is it I never stay to do just one thing? Why can't I be like others and stay put?" Again I felt like the odd one out and wondered what was wrong with me. Over time I discovered it's not about sticking to one modality, it's about learning everything there is, so I can encompass the whole of what I have learnt and bring that knowledge to my clients. I am not fixed into just one way of thinking: if a situation feels right for Psychosynthesis then I will talk about it, or I will draw on my knowledge of yoga or meditation, I bring in whatever is called for. I have found being bound to one way of teaching can leave you blinkered and inclined to think just that one way. So now I am happy to keep learning and bringing broad and varied wisdom to my clients as is fitting. This is where the mind does its real job, helping us learn, finding new knowledge, and opening up our minds to all wondrous ideas. Knowledge and learning are the key to moving to forward as well, everything is joined. We have heart; go inside find your true self, move forward. We have mind; learn, experience, gain knowledge, again move forward. We have our third eye which encompasses all. All three are joined together, in balance, the way it should be. When they are all in balance everything in our life's flow, when they are not we are out of harmony and everything goes against us, life is a battlefield.

I love music. It is wonderful and feeds the soul in so many different ways. One of my favourite singers is Garth Brooks. When I put on his CD I just turn the stereo up full blast, and sing at the top of my lungs. One day I was listening to him and he sang a song about how he thanked God for unanswered prayers, "Just because he doesn't answer doesn't mean he doesn't care, some of God's greatest gifts are unanswered prayers." Suddenly the words just hit home and, of course, made so much sense. I looked back on all the times I had prayed and asked God for something, but I wasn't really asking for something for me, I just didn't see it at that time. So I came to realise that, if it is in our best interest, then we do get what we pray for, but if it isn't, then we don't. At times it will also seem like God isn't there but, later when you look back, when you look at the bigger picture, you can then see he was there all along, just not as you expected. That realisation was a light bulb going on moment. I have certainly had a few of them over the years!

I remember, when I was about thirteen, my brother was hit by a pellet gun. We had a policeman come to the house to ask questions about the incident. In that moment I got it in my head I wanted to become a policewoman. So that was what I started to work towards. At fifteen I applied to join the Metropolitan Cadets when I turned sixteen. They were based in London and offered basic training which led into policing when you reached eighteen. I went through all the tests thinking I stood a pretty good chance of getting in. When I was at boarding school mum called to say I hadn't been accepted as my eyesight wasn't good enough, but I could reapply when I was eighteen. She then carried on to say she believed I was too thick to be accepted anyway. I was even more surprised when she continued to say dad also believed I was thick. Talk about a double blow. There I was reeling from the words and the implications of the call. My dreams were shattered and I had been kicked in the teeth by my mum as well; both of which knocked my confidence and those words stuck with me for a very long time. After all, you don't expect to be told by your parents you're thick. I think I was more devastated that dad had such a low opinion me, as I always thought he believed in me. Comments like these were not uncommon in my family. My brother had always been the target, and it looked as if they were starting to come my way too.

I did always wonder why I never got in, and, more importantly, why my parents never supported me. It took me a long time to recover. I never applied to the Police again as I knew my eyes wouldn't change when I was eighteen. Later, when I was looking at possibilities for careers, I looked at the Army and thought I could be Policewomen there. I even had a look around the offices at a local base. As I walked around I kept thinking, "This could be for me." However, that idea stayed at the back burner and never eventuated as I got into nursing instead. It was only when I started nursing that my mum said, "You can't be that thick after all!" I was twenty.

When I look back at this time, I can now see why I wasn't meant to get into the police as the work would have made me shut down even more emotionally. Dealing with criminals and seeing the harsher side of life would have been totally wrong for me. It would have confirmed to me that life is harsh. I would have needed to be tough and show no emotion just to survive. Instead, through nursing, I got to see the gentler and more caring side of life, which helped to bring out the softer side of me. Nursing also started to show me about emotions. Of course, it is only now I can see that, back then I was devastated I didn't get into the Police Force. So you see sometimes it is good we don't get what we ask for!

## Chapter Five
## Nursing days

*Look at the brighter side of life, see the funnier side of life,
and you will feel much better for it.*

Before I got into nursing I had various jobs that each
lasted no longer than six months. I worked as a barmaid,
shop assistant and clerical assistant, but none of them
held any weight with me; I would get bored and move
on. One day I went to visit my brother in hospital. He
had been sick since he was about six months old. He had
some type of auto-immune deficiency, a rarity my parents
were told. His body was unable to produce calcium when
he was a baby and as he got older his glands became less
functional too. So we were frequent visitors to hospitals.
One day I was talking to the nurse who was looking after
him to find out what she did in her job. As she talked
about her work I thought, "That sounds alright as a job,"
so she gave me a name and address of a person who
worked in enrolments, and I applied for nursing. On the
application form I had to explain why I wanted to
become a Nurse. I stumbled at this point and wondered
what on earth could I put as talking to a nurse didn't
seem to be a feasible enough reason. So, after a little
thought, I talked about my brother and told his story of
being such a frequent patient (and a model one at that). I

got accepted and it was because of my brother I got into nursing.

I didn't realise at that time, however, there were two types of Nurse: Registered and Enrolled, and I didn't know the difference. It so happened the Nurse I was talking to was an Enrolled Nurse and I had been accepted to train as an Enrolled Nurse.

My very first day in college was daunting to say the least; everyone had some type of basic nursing training whether from working in a nursing home, or from completing a pre nursing course. But not me, I was as new as the dawn and had never done any kind of nursing. I remember wondering what had I let myself in for. At the start of our training we were in college for about six or eight weeks learning the basics, and then we were let loose on the wards for three months. For my first rotation I was on a busy medical ward at the Royal Infirmary in Edinburgh, and I had been assigned to the Sister! "Great!' I thought, "No pressure then!" I was petrified. Sisters back then were very stern, you weren't allowed to sit and talk with a patient; you had to be doing something. The only time you were allowed to sit down was at the end your shift to write your notes up.

One of the first things she asked me to do was to get a commode from the sluice. Well, she could have spoken in Dutch and I would probably have understood more of what she was saying. I had no idea what I was meant to be doing. I went running to the top of the ward thinking, "Commode? Sluice? What are they? Where are they?" Thankfully, I saw another Nurse who told me where the sluice was. It turned out a commode is a portable toilet can be wheeled to patient bedsides. I of course, came back with just the bedpan and not the commode. In the end Sister had to go and get it herself. That was my first day.

After my first three month rotation, I was blown away when the Sister said to let her know if I wanted to come back and work on her ward after I had qualified! "I couldn't have been that bad after all!" I thought. I still remember her words as if it was yesterday. To have the Sister ask me back was a major boost for my confidence. Never before had anyone said well done, or given words of encouragement. Yet here was the Sister in Charge offering me work, who had only known me for three months!

Then we went back to College for another two week stint of training. It stayed like that for the remainder of the course, two weeks College, followed by three month placement on the wards. I worked on many wards including Surgical, Physically Disabled and Orthopaedics. I enjoyed all of them but it was always daunting starting a new modality or working on a different ward, but each experience was great learning. In the early days of my training I was still the novice and seemed to say the wrong thing. Once, in College, we each had to take the head tutor's blood pressure as practice. It came to my turn and I went through the steps. I told her what I had measured her blood pressure at. "Rubbish," she said, "it's never that high." I took it again, but it was still the same. This time I told her I could hear her pulse! She told me I had it all wrong; that what I could feel was not her pulse. She made me feel very uncomfortable and I squirmed out of College that day. To this day, I still swear the reading I had for her blood pressure was right, but was it any wonder it had risen after teaching us!

My very first day working at the Physically Disabled Unit was really daunting and terrifying. As I arrived on the ward, the staff nurse on duty for the night was struggling to control one of the patients. He came down the stairs, saw me, grabbed my head and banged it on the wall. I was petrified and kept thinking, "Oh my god, what have I come to?" The patient then managed to bite the nurse through quite a few layers of clothing; the staff nurse had to go for a tetanus shot. Nothing like that first day happened again during my time on the ward and it turned out to be my best placement ever and I just loved the staff and patients. Sadly, in recent years the facility was closed down.

My training was rewarding and hilarious at the same time. It was not unusual for disaster to strike during my last day on a ward. On my last day on Surgical Ward I broke my fingers by dropping two metal bedpans on them. I felt very foolish having to sit outside Accident and Emergency as a nurse. I managed to flood the kitchen during my last day on the Orthopaedic Ward. As I tried to turn the hot water urn off, I was instead turning it on. Water gushed everywhere. Initially, I quietly called for assistance, but as it was getting worse I was screaming, "HELP!" I had a huge flood to clean up that day. I have no idea why something always happened on my last day on a ward, but it does make you wonder how I managed to stay in nursing for twenty seven years!

With whatever I have done in my life, I have always believed I would achieve good things. I have always had high expectations and dreamed of life being wonderful. One day, however, I was visiting my aunt, and was all excited about my nurses training. I admit I often get carried away with my thoughts and my plans for the future. As I talked about my training, I told her one day I would be in charge of a ward. "Don't be silly," she said, "you're too thick and besides, you're only an Enrolled Nurse. Talk about being knocked down from a great height; my family had a great way of doing that to me.

Years later I did in fact run a Children's Outpatients Department, so I did end up in charge of a ward after all. I could have applied for the Charge Nurse position on the ward but chose to work in the Outpatients Department instead. By this time I had completed further training to become a Registered Sick Children's Nurse.

I look back at my training and am always grateful I trained as an Enrolled Nurse before qualifying as a Sick Children's Nurse. Enrolled Nurses are pivotal in caring for patients as they do a lot of basic care and have a hand on approach, which every patient needs. Would I have done it all differently? Absolutely not. My experience as an Enrolled Nurse was the backbone of my nursing career and one I certainly wouldn't change.

My decision to do my Sick Children's training was the result of a few incidents in my career which involved children. Soon after qualifying as an Enrolled Nurse I joined the Royal Air Force as a nurse. I was a Senior Aircraftwoman or SACW for short. I was stationed in Ely, Cambridgeshire, England. One weekend I was in charge of the Children's Ward. There wasn't anything serious happening on the ward, so everything should have been okay. However, towards the end of the shift we were expecting to admit a child suffering from asthma. While I waited for the Doctor to arrive, I was busy doing the paperwork and preparing for the admission. When the Doctor arrived all hell broke loose. He was shouting and swearing as he ordered me to get things. He was also demanding to know why certain things hadn't been done before the boy's arrival. I now know I had misunderstood the seriousness of the boy's condition. When I went home after my shift, I never slept as I kept worrying about the boy.

By the next day the boy's condition had improved. On the Monday, when everyone was back to work, my roster was changed and I was no longer in charge. Not one person spoke to me about what had happened or explained to me why the roster had been changed. All I know is the Doctor shouted at the Charge Nurse and then the changes to the roster were made. I felt personally responsible for that situation, and held the guilt inside me for a long time, believing it had been my entirely fault. It's easy to feel guilty in situations like this when, for your whole life, you are told you are no good or you are too thick. Not long after I was posted to Germany, but the move didn't bring any closure; as that incident was still hanging over my head like a ton weight.

I was in the Air Force for four years. Originally I joined up for nine, but knew I wouldn't do the full time. After leaving the Air Force I worked in the big smoke of London. I started off working on a private ward at a Neurosurgical Hospital. Directly behind the hospital was Great Ormond Street Hospital for Children. At this stage I was getting bored with the direction I was heading and actually contemplated leaving nursing due to big changes around this time that meant Enrolled Nurses could no longer be in charge. So, if I wanted to stay in nursing I knew I had to become a Registered Nurse, but I also knew I didn't want to go down that path. However, I soon realised I could do my training and specialize in working with children. So I applied to train as a Sick Children's Nurse at Great Ormond Street and was accepted to the course.

I was not new to nursing when I started my second time round at College, but I had only worked in the field of children for a maximum of six months and everyone else in the class had come directly from a children's ward. As I had come from a busy adult Neuro Surgical ward, again, I felt out of my depth but knew I was driven to be there. I was still haunted by memories of the boy with asthma, but knew it was time to face the ghosts of the past.

I was working on a medical ward and I was caring for a very sick child with asthma. At first I kept saying to the Staff Nurse in Charge, I didn't think I was capable of looking after the child. Thankfully, she had every confidence in me and reminded me I was more than capable and she would be right there if needed. I cared for that child very successfully, was able to put an old haunt to rest. I was grateful to that nurse for having confidence in me. I had combated my fear about caring for children with asthma by ensuring I was never left in that situation again without the proper training. It felt great and I was proud of myself.

During my training one of the subjects discussed was abuse. Nothing new there I thought, everyone is aware of physical and sexual abuse. Then it came to the discussion of emotional abuse. I had never heard of the concept before. It was quite new to me. During one of the lectures I thought I was going to have to walk out. I was getting really upset and angry; I was fidgety, couldn't settle and my head was shouting, "Come on, get me out of here." I burst into tears in the toilets after the lecture. I was almost hysterical. I had related to every single example of emotional abuse that had been given. It was as if the lecturer had used me as an example. What I realised in that lecture was what I thought was normal as I was growing up had in fact been emotional abuse. Things like, "you are stupid," "you are no good," and "you won't amount to anything," I thought were normal. I was never given any praise, by no means received any encouragement.

I know now I was emotionally abused by my family. One time really stuck with me. When I was fifteen I wanted some advice on what exams to take, so I asked mum for help. Her reply was, "Go away! I have enough problems of my own without having yours." If I remember rightly, dad hadn't come back from the pub yet and she was stressed, as she always was when he was late. Whenever I asked for help it was generally met with the same response. So, after numerous rejections, I stopped asking and haven't asked ever since.

I realised everything that was said about emotional abuse in the lecture, the examples of negative things that can be said, all the put downs, could have been about me. I was left wondering, "What do I do about this? How do I cope with this knowledge?" It was because of the lecture I started having counselling, but up until then I had always thought counselling was only for people who were desperate and really depressed. Boy was I wrong.

That was my introduction to emotional abuse. All abuse is horrendous and no one should ever have to experience it. Sadly, the reality is most people will probably be subjected to some form of abuse in their lifetime. As we all know children grow up to become adults. If we don't have the right role models as children, how can we be expected to do things differently when we are an adult? Without positive role models the cycle of abuse keeps going, handed down from generation to generation. To break the cycle, the abuse has to be acknowledged and it must be agreed it is no longer acceptable behaviour. Knowing there is a different way to do things is the start of change. We don't have to put up with abuse just because it comes from family members, even if it has always been that way. That start and change can happen by when we take control of our own lives and say, "No more." When we start to go inside ourselves, and do our own inner work, we change, and then we can stop the cycle of abuse from continuing.

Each generation is different. It has only been in the last thirty to forty years that a lot of research around how we treat children has been done. Before that, children were always seen, but not heard. Children had no rights. They were expected to do as they are told and not to ask questions. Certainly my parents would have been brought up like that. Both my grandparents were extremely strict. They had their own beliefs which all family members had to take on, whether they wanted to or not. This was the same in most families. In many ways things are changing with each generation, but many people are still bitter and resent how they were brought up. This is our time now to change all that, and we can, but we have to choose exactly what it is we want to change. We no longer need to be victims of generational abuse; we need to stop that cycle.

After learning about emotional abuse, I went through a huge range of emotions: anger, blame, shame; poor me, why me......and on it went. Every time I saw my mum I was horrible to her, thinking if I was mean enough she would ask, "What's wrong?" but she never did and I continued being horrible. I tried really hard to get a reaction from her. The only time she would react would be if my younger brother annoyed her. Rather than pull him up, she would turn around to me and have a go at the way I was behaving without ever asking me what was wrong. She would only ever react to me because of my younger brother's behaviour. This left me not knowing what to say, and what's more, I didn't know how to say anything about how I was feeling. I was angry and we weren't a family that talked about issues and emotions, we just blamed. So I dealt with it the only way I knew how. I drank and had a good time. Well, I pretended I was having a good time, but realistically I was falling apart inside and didn't know how to stop it. I was a tender age of twenty eight when all this happened.

I managed to continue with the course, while, at the same time dealing with all the emotions I had coming up. I look back now and see how synchronicity really does work. It really all is about timing. It was through working with children that my issues started to come up. I wouldn't have been ready to face them before then, as I would still probably have been in denial. But there really is a time for everything. We just need to have courage to face it and change it.

It wasn't until I had my own daughter I could see how my mum managed what was happening in a different light. From time to time I can hear myself repeating the same things my mum used to say and I have to stop myself. Sometimes, if I get a little short with my daughter, I wonder what it must have been like for mum. She had three children and a husband who was very unsupportive, drank a lot, and had no time for his children. She practically brought us up by herself.

Whenever my dad was away with the Army, he would bring back a gift for us. I always thought it was great that dad did this and looked forward to him coming home. Years later I found out he never did anything of the sort; mum got them. It just showed to me he never thought about us when he was away, so why would he buy us a gift. At Christmas time it was always mum who got the presents. She would save all year and got no money had from dad. I know men might not be involved a lot in day to day family things, but at least they can have an input at times. My dad never did, he was too busy drinking or thinking about himself.

Once I remember I turned on dad and challenged him over the fact he never did anything for us. He didn't play with the boys, take us anywhere, or show any interest in what we were doing. I was really angry with him and told him so. He had tears in his eyes. I don't think we spoke for a few weeks after that. I would walk out the living room every time he walked in. Even after everything I had said, nothing changed, absolutely nothing. He would lie on the settee and ask one of us to get him the ashtray, or get this or that. He never did anything for himself. I used to have to do his ironing, which initially I was happy to do but, as I got older, I started to realise he was taking advantage of us and it was all take with him. He never gave anything back to us.

One thing dad never did was talk, ever. The only time he would was when he had been drinking, and then you couldn't shut him up. He used to go on and on about the same situation. Not shouting, just rambling really. It always made me feel uncomfortable, I never liked it. That used to really annoy me as he couldn't be bothered to talk to us when he was sober, but when he was drunk he wouldn't stop. That hurt a lot. I remember thinking I would never do the same thing when I was an adult. Well, best intentions in the world don't always happen. Without a doubt I was heading down the same road as my dad with drinking. I knew it, but how could I change it? I also swore I would never drink. Again, that never happened as I was always in social situations where there was a lot of alcohol. So it was normal to drink. So, as a child, I had all the best intentions but some never worked out. I was repeating the same pattern my dad did, and that was scary. I was forced to make changes through circumstances that happened. I still had a choice and if I had wanted too I could have refused. I chose change, my dad decided not to; he stayed a victim of his own story.

My dad went from living at home with his parents to getting married and then joining the Army. So he always had people to look after him. Once he asked his parents to get him out of the Army but he was told by his grandmother, "You have made your bed, now lie in it." I think it's a horrible saying but it's one that was used a lot in those days. Not long after I had been born mum went to her parents to ask for help, I am guessing to come home I'm not really sure. All I do know is she got told the same thing, "You have made your bed, now lie in it." There was no sense of compassion and no offer of help. Before that though, mum knew she didn't want to get married when she was in the church on her wedding day! Obviously she didn't pull out.

How many times has that happened to people, they have known that they shouldn't be doing something, but do it anyway. They are going against their own instinct by not having enough belief in themselves. From my experience, following your instinct never lets you down; it works with you not against you. The consequences of mum not following her instinct didn't just affect her; eventually it would affect three children as well. I often wondered what life would have been like if mum had left dad when she had wanted to. But then, would I be the person I am today? It's hard to know the answer to that as it is our experiences that shape us, and certainly these experiences shaped me. So, would I have wanted to change things? As a child I would have answered, "Yes!" hands down, "Give me different parents." Now, as an adult with a child of my own, having had the experiences I have, and with a bit more understanding about the process of life, then probably not. Young children love their parents no matter what they do. I did for a while, but as I grew up that started to change. That's why, when the chance came to go to boarding school, I jumped at it.

# Chapter Six
## Children should be heard

*Everything is as it should be.*

Quite often when I sit down to meditate I get shown or have a feeling that there is something I need to do. One such moment happened on a full moon in 2012. I had gathered three other women who were keen to go down to the river and do a little ceremony. For centuries women have suffered many atrocities for numerous reasons, and sadly this is still occurring in some countries today. Women have always been classed as the nurtures, midwives and healers who have worked to help heal the land as well. Women have a connection with the earth, which is also classed as a mother. Yet women have also been persecuted, burnt, hanged and raped over the centuries just for being women. The little ceremony in 2012 was about claiming back what is rightfully ours, our own feminine power. Many women have forgotten this power, and it has been hidden deep down inside of us. There are many different layers of "rubbish" covering the power. The rubbish stops us from accessing what is rightfully ours: our knowledge and wisdom.

On the night it was really interesting as I almost didn't think we would be able to do the ceremony. It was extremely windy, in fact we had not had winds like that in a long time but, thankfully, the winds settled down and so we carried on. We connected with Mother Earth and Father Sky in our own way. We danced, sang and moved in all sorts of directions. It felt very invigorating and we knew we were getting back in touch with our true selves. We were moving beyond the fear of what had happened to us in the past. We were reclaiming our memory and starting to wake up. We let go of the past but also remembered and honoured, where we had come from.

We each have feminine and male energy in us, as we have a physical mother and father to help create us. Depending on our sex will be the dominant energy, so a female will be more dominant in feminine energy. Over the centuries the feminine energy has been dormant as the male energy has been in control. The male energy is predominantly about taking charge and establishing order, this is sometimes done by creating fear in the masses. The feminine energy, its principal role is about love and healing. Healing of the individual and healing of the land. We are at a stage in our evolution, that, as human beings we need to be aware of the changes we need to make so that this is possible. We now need to bring both feminine and male energies back into balance. To function well we need both energies to be in sync with each other, not one being dominant as it has been in the past.

Everything in life is about balance. Our body is designed that if any system gets out of balance it tries to correct itself, but, most of the time we do not allow that to happen as we are too busy! We need dark to help us sleep, we can't be in light all the time, and we need balance. Hence, there is no difference when it comes to female and male energies. We need both, they need to be in balance with each other. All we have to do is look back at history to see what has happened with the male energies being dominant. Of course before that happened it was the feminine energy that was dominant, but again that wasn't too healthy either as it was all one way! Everything is about balance and so this time round we need both working together, united. Now is the time for love and acceptance of others. To reach a state of love and acceptance we each have to go inside ourselves and let go of all the old hurts we are hiding, this goes for males as well. We need to consciously connect with both the female and male energies that we are. To help us move forward into the future we also need to reconnect with where we have come from.

As always it takes a while for the penny to drop. I talk about everything being in need of balance, joining together. I have also said how timing is important and that as therapist we need to do the work ourselves first. Recently I finally understood, I had another light bulb moment. I had actually needed to join my male side. I had disregarded it for a very long time; I probably kidded myself that my male side was fine, when in fact I was completely ignoring it. I was able to rectify that once I had realised, so you see we are very good at fooling ourselves. Finally I was able to actually grasp what it meant by being in balance.

Growing up as a child wasn't easy; actually I don't think it is ever simple for any child to grow up. We have to do as we are told and ask no questions; certainly that was the case when I was growing up. I had two younger brothers with three and ten years between us. I was close to the one in the middle as there was only three years between us, my youngest brother, I thought was spoilt. He would have tantrums, which is not unusual for children, but when he had one my mother would always give into him. As an eleven or twelve year old I knew that response wasn't right, but he always got his own way. He was the only one of us who ever had a birthday party or a birthday cake. I didn't have my first birthday cake until I was sixteen year old and it wasn't even made by my mum, it came from my aunty who lived in England at the time. She knew I had never had one so made it especially for me; I was totally chuffed and felt like I had won the lottery. My brother in the middle was always being told he wouldn't come to anything; he was sick most of his life. Then when my younger brother came along, we both got compared to him. We were told that he was the brainy one and that he would be the only child who would ever amount to anything. Words like that used to hurt, and what we had to live with them all the time. Neither I nor my brother could change that. When you constantly hear things like that, over time you start to shut down emotionally as a way of keeping yourself safe, and that is what I did. It always seemed that mum had time for my youngest brother and not for her two other children. She once told me that if she had my younger brother first she wouldn't have had either me or my other brother. I once reminded her of this, but she denied having said it. But as far as I am concerned, this is certainly something that no child would forget being told because she was basically she's saying that she didn't want my brother and I. Words like this create emotion that we hold onto and we tend to bury such emotions deep inside of us, hoping to forget them and certainly not deal with them. That's exactly what I did, I buried those emotions. I have no doubt that mum would have been told something similar herself as a child, so she kept the cycle going by repeating the words to me. But this is where the cycle stops – with me.

Why is it that when it comes to family we are expected to take whatever they might throw at us? They can use and abuse us and yet we say, "That's okay, they're family. They're allowed!" really? Should they be allowed to abuse others just because they are family? Personally, I don't think so. We don't put up with abuse from friends, so why do we tolerate it from family. If a friend treated us the same way then I am sure we would no longer be friends with them. Yet, with family we make excuses and overlook their behaviour because that's what expected of us. One of my aunts, who I hadn't seen to or spoken to in about twenty years, was in Australia and thought it was okay for her to come and see me in New Zealand. I guess that's fair enough, but she wanted to come for the birth of my daughter. I said no, for many reasons, but the main one was I had no idea how I was going to be or feel with the birth. The last thing I needed was to have a family member who thought it was her right to be present because she was family. If our situation had been different, in that we talked often and had a good relationship, then I am sure it would have been different.

Then my daughter was about three months old and we were coming back from New Zealand. My aunt was keen to meet up, but the only time we had was at the airport as we had a three hour drive back and Lyndsay was working the next day. I suggested meeting at the airport, but again that didn't go down well as I never heard back from her. Not long after this my aunt asked mum to stop sending her pictures of my daughter as she didn't want to know or have anything to do with her. Did I feel guilty at what had happened? Well no, I felt within my rights to refuse her, but I doubt from the way she reacted that she understands that. When I was a child we did get on, but that changed when I stayed with her as a teenager. Growing up she was always my favourite aunty, so I jumped at the chance to stay with her at weekends when I was at boarding school, I thought it would be great. Slowly, over time that started to change. Partly, I was a teenager! But it seemed that every chance she had I would get put down, nothing I would do was right. Now, I had this all my life at home, I really didn't expect to get it from my aunt as well. So I stopped going as I no longer felt comfortable or welcome. We still haven't talked about any of that to this day!

Even after all the work I had been doing on myself, from time to time I would have moments of feeling sorry for myself, feeling really low with everything getting me down. Yet, as a result of the work I had been doing, they didn't last as long and I was getting quicker at recognizing them and dealing with them. It is generally in one of these moments I will have what I call a "light bulb" moment. For a long time I had thought that it was my adult self who was helping my inner child, as she was stuck. In fact it's been the other way round; it's been my inner child trying to help my adult self. As children we are pretty resilient and cope with most things, including what is done to us. Children are very trusting, no matter what happens. When it comes to the emotional side of things, unless children are shown how to deal with their emotions they will hide them away. Yet children are always forgiving, it is only as we start to head into teenage years I presume things change. As teenagers we start to realise the world isn't the place what we thought it was; we are starting to lose our innocence I guess. That's when the adult self, which is less forgiving, will start to kick in, and now we start to blame.

Over the years I have done a lot of work around the inner child and have struggled every single time. I have fought tooth and nail, but whatever is there has not wanted to surface. I have prepared assignments and talked to my inner child, who at first was too shy to even come out and talk. I have had many healing sessions for her. I have also participated in soul recovery sessions, and during the very last one, my inner child came back to me. Interestingly though, it was only half of her and she had been hidden in a cave. After this session I struggled with accepting her back and had to have a session around it with Jay. Initially all was well and I felt quite at peace knowing that my inner child was finally back. Remember I said only half of her had come back. I didn't see the importance of that at the time, but in a meditation some years later I was shown that my inner child was now ready to fully come back. All this time I had thought she was present, but often wondered why I was struggled to have fun knowing my inner child was there. I put it down to my inner child not knowing how to have fun, when in fact, it was only half of her, and so she wasn't quite complete. As I look at it now I had always thought the healing was centred on the inner child from this lifetime. But in fact, depending on how many lives we have led, will determine which inner child we have to heal. So yes, I had been healing my inner child, but not necessarily the one from this lifetime. We can only heal when those parts of us needing to be healed are ready. We can't push or force healing to go fast as that would cause such a big upset that our systems wouldn't be able to handle it. It would be like overloading a circuit with energy to the point of explosion; the same thing would happen with us, we would retreat back into ourselves if we forced what wasn't ready to come.

As a child we were never allowed in until tea time so I played outside most of the time. Times are different today and many children are very rarely outside. Today there is more awareness of what is deemed safe and not safe for children to do. Some modern parents have moved away from the way they were brought up. If their parents were really strict, they seem to do the opposite today and some children have no clear boundaries as a result. Too strict is not healthy but neither is not having any boundaries. Children need to know where they stand. They will push boundaries and try the limits—that is their job, but still need help and guidance in this crazy world. It's like anything, balance is best. Children need to be able to explore for themselves but they also need to know what is acceptable and what isn't; everything within its limits but not controlling. As an adult I find myself hibernating inside, away from people. As a child I had no choice but to be outside, so it seems I am doing the complete opposite as an adult by staying inside. Neither is too healthy, and I am working on changing that. Actually, having my daughter has helped create more balance here. As she takes part in certain activities I have to leave the house and find myself in places where there are other people which forces me out of my comfort zone. Do I like this? Of course I don't but it's something I have to do for the sake of my daughter. I am, however, getting better at trusting my own judgment and know when something feels safe or not. Just from being around other people, I'm not necessarily taking on their problems as my own, something I would have done not so long ago. I also don't take it personally if they don't speak, as I would have previously. I am starting to feel comfortable with who I am as a person, and trust my own judgments. I no longer go to that place where I think everything is my fault. I can start to see things objectively without being emotionally involved. This is a huge achievement.

My daughter is a great teacher in her own right. If we take the time to watch any child we would realise they are all teachers. Often however, adults tend to think, "We are the adult and they are the child. What do they know?" Never underestimate a child, their wisdom, their love, their kindness. They say the most profound, yet very true statements. The phrase, "out of the mouths of babes," rings true to me as children possess the greatest of wisdom in the most innocent way. Children are also great judges of characters. They know when a person isn't right, and they can sense when something is wrong. Yet sometimes, because of their ability to trust so much they can get led astray.

What if we were to turn the concept of learning around, in that children would be the teachers and the adults would be the learners? What would that look like and how would that go? I am sure it would not go very well for some adults as they would struggle with the concept of learning from children. Yet if we do accept that children have a lot to teach us, then it could be that children are here to help adults heal. If so, would that change how society looks upon and treats children? I'd certainly like to think it so, but understand not all adults are ready to see and receive healing and learning from children. All adults are hurt and wounded regardless of what they say; the hurt is hidden deep within, and to heal we just need to gently allow it to come to the surface. As adults we don't necessarily need to know everything, do everything "my" way or have full control. We only want to control things now as we never had any power when we were children and we felt helpless, so we compensate for this as adults by trying to control everything. Our children are the next generation, if we want it to change for them we need to make the changes in ourselves now. By doing this we can stop the generational cycle of abuse that is very damaging.

Stop for a second and really watch and listen to your children. What are they trying to show or tell you? Are you brave enough to follow a child's guidance? I know I certainly do. I don't always get it right, but I know when I need to listen to my daughter and act on what she says. Having the trust to do this has only come about from all the work I have been doing on myself over the years. I am doubtful I would have been able to be guided by a child if I hadn't done this work as I would have been stuck in the adult way of thinking, "I'm the adult, you are the child." I try to let my daughter do what she needs to. But even this freedom is limited by considerations for things such as safety.

When we make decisions about the safety of children, I wonder if we restrict their activities based on our adult knowledge of the worst that can happen. Perhaps, however, we should allow them to do what they want. This is where it gets really hard to balance what we should and shouldn't let them do, for if they are connected with their guides, and all children are, then there are lessons in everything they want to do. This makes it hard as we want to keep our children safe, but maybe it is our own fears putting them at risk. I don't know the answer as this is a really big issue and one that will need a lot of debate. If I disagree with something my daughter has done generally it means there is an old issue I have that needs to be addressed; this happens a lot. I have to figure out what it is and sometimes it takes a few days for me to do that. So, with best intentions in the world, I don't always make the right decision at that time. For me, the most important thing I can do is tell my daughter every day how much I love her, talk to her if I am grumpy and tell her so she knows my mood hasn't anything to do with her; so no blame on her part. She is her own person and she has her own agenda for being here in the world at this time. What that is I don't know, but hopefully I can help support whatever it is by being open to everything. Without a doubt children still need guidance and help from adults, but adults need to come from a perspective of love and reassurance, not fear and control.

It's not someone or something that holds us back, even though we think it is. It's the emotion attached to it. Most of us think we think are our emotions. We identify with them, we stay with them, but we actually need to disassociate from all emotions, even the ones we are holding onto. Most of the time we have no idea what emotions we are holding onto, but we don't get into adulthood without having a lot of hang-ups or emotional distress somewhere in our life. We are all told to "carry on," "don't go there, it's in the past" or "leave the past behind." To some extent this is good advice, but not if it is the past, and the associated emotion, that is preventing us from moving forward. If that is the case, then we do need to look at the past. Most people, however, are scared at what they might find, remember or have to change and, for some, that is just too difficult and they don't want to go there.

When we are caught up in our own emotions it is hard to shift them; we are stuck in them. A situation needs to change, before our emotions can change. When you are anxious, you may recognize it, but find it hard to change the feeling. For change to take place, half the battle is recognizing the emotion then, and perhaps more challenging, is to change it. But how do you actually change emotions and feelings? It's like using positive affirmations to help you change things in your life. To some degree they are useful, but it takes more than just saying words for change to take place. The key to success is to actually believe in what you say; you must feel what you say and then you take action on it. Don't expect to just sit back and speak positive words and if you really don't feel it; you are wasting your time and only fooling yourself, things won't change. It is easy when using this approach to blame the affirmations for not working when things don't change. For affirmations to work you must believe in the words and feel them within. As you become more aware of your emotions and how they affect you, you will start to see a change in how you react differently to situations. When you make a positive change you can see and feel it in a healthy loving way. As you change so do the people around you, which is even better.

I have stopped many a time while trying to write this chapter. I have been finding it hard and my fear about writing this book has been holding me back. The writing is not only bringing up old issues I thought I had dealt with, but I am putting my life out there in the open arena for all to see. Emotionally, that is hard for me as all my life I have been trying to fit in, while knowing deep down I was different and didn't really want to fit in. But socially I felt I had to "blend," so I went against my own guidance, as I didn't know enough about intuition then. Slowly, over time, I was drowning in my own lack of courage, strength and conviction to follow what I knew I should have been doing. For over twenty years I ignored my true path and ignored my own guidance. At the age of about six or seven I had been shown that for twenty odd years I would be lost, rebel against everyone and everything and not be happy, but after that time everything would be okay, as would I be okay. I had forgotten about all of that until I was in my forties when I had a flashback. I started to remember what I had been shown as a child, I had the feeling I had always known about this and knew in my heart that what I had seen was true. Why then did I forget all I had been shown? If I had remembered, would I have changed the way I did things over the years? In every situation we all have a choice and maybe I had to make the choices I did to help me get where I am today. How different would things have been if I had followed my own instinct? I don't really know the answer to that, but I do know the experiences we have will either make or break us, depending on what happens and how we deal with it. As children, our parents and families play a huge role in choices made for us and it is only when we reach adulthood that, if we want to, we can change how we approach things.

As difficult as it is, I know I need to write this book. I know I am attached to emotions and I need to let go of them for myself and in order to help others. But boy there are so many lessons out there for each of us. To live this life we need to walk the walk and talk the talk. Remember that old saying, "Do what I say, not what I do." Well it is only partly true. To actually do what we say, to put into action what we say is also important. After all, how can we change if we do don't feel it, think it and action it? For change to happen we need to do all three. Like anything in life, it's about maintaining balance in everything we do.

## Chapter Seven
## Two of my angels

*Honour your inner self and everything else in your life will flow as it should.*

In my twenty-seven years as a nurse I have looked after some amazing people, from the very first patient I looked after who died, to the last patient I cared for, who had just given birth. In between them, there are too many patients to mention. But there are two who I need to talk about as they were very special people and both have touched me in ways I never expected. For to me they were both my angels and still are.

The first patient I looked after was when I worked in London in a private ward in a NHS hospital. I'm not using her name as I haven't got permission from her family, but it was twenty three years ago when I cared for her. She came from Africa and walked into the hospital with her husband. It was obvious right from the start they were both amazing people. The love they had for each other was evident from the moment they walked into the ward. After surgery she was left paralyzed with a tracheostomy (a tube placed in the throat to help her breathe) so she was not able to speak or move. Along with other nurses I cared for her over an eighteen month period. She was quite a challenge so not many nurses liked looking after her, but another nurse and I had a soft spot for her and she became our favourite patient. So, whenever we were on duty, we always cared for her. It was really hard for her to accept what had happened as she had come into hospital with the hope of having the tumour removed, but sadly there were complications during the operation; a risk she and her husband had known about. Not being able to communicate was hard for her as she had been a nurse herself in her own country. However, she found her own unique way of communicating through her eyes and body instead, and as a result you always knew what kind of mood she was in when you walked into the room. Sometimes caring for her was very challenging, especially if she was not in a very good mood. However, there were also some very caring moments we shared while doing some of the smallest of jobs. Even when she was at her most challenging I would wonder on those occasions how would I feel if the situation was reversed. This always helped me get things back into perspective.

Her husband was a joy whenever he visited. Sometimes he would be away with work, which he never liked, as he hated leaving her side, but needs must be. You could tell she also hated when he was away and she would always be a bit more emotional whenever he came back, but happy. On returning he would come bearing gifts: pineapples for the staff, and lots of other things he knew she loved, it was amazing. I was not used to such generosity, but being a private ward this was allowed at the time. He would always ask how she had been in his absence and was very attentive to her when he arrived back, not leaving her side. Sometimes they would put on a video of her made before she came to England and we got to see what she was like before the surgery. She was amazing; full of life and bubbly. We could see from the outset she was very proud of her four children and her husband and her family was her life. Whenever the video was put on tears would run down her face. It was lovely to see, but, at the same time, very sad. Numerous visitors came to see her and there was always plenty of laughter in her room. As I said she was an amazing person who had oodles of love; there was definitely something very special about her.

I was due to leave the ward to do my Sick Children's Registered Nurse Training Course and was on night duty for my last shift. She had been unwell for a few nights with a chest infection and on my last night she took a turn for the worse. There were a few relatives in the room and of course her husband. He just kept looking at me and saying, "She'll be okay, won't she?" I tried to reassure him but had a gut feeling her condition wasn't good. It wasn't; she deteriorated quickly and within a few hours she had passed away. The grief that came from that room after her death was unimaginable. There was howling, screaming and so much noise. I had never witnessed anything like it before and I didn't know what to do. I remember going into the drug room and just standing there in total shock and feeling numb. In the end she had died so quickly. The emotions I was experiencing were new to me and I didn't know what to do with them. I stayed in the drug room for a while, leaving the family to their grief. One of the nurses came in to see how I was and asked if I wanted someone else to prepare the body. I had always cared for her so felt I had to be the one to carry out the final care. The family left for a while so I returned to her room. I was shaking as I entered but what I saw and experienced that night when I walked back into the room will stay with me until I draw my last breath. There was a sense of peacefulness as I walked in. I walked up to her and just stood for a few minutes beside her. In death she looked so very peaceful, serene and had a smile on her face. I had not seen that smile while she had been in hospital. From the look on her face it was clear as day that at last she was at peace and she was happy. This realisation blew me away as I had never seen that before, ever. I had been wondering how I was going to get through this final job of caring for her, and there she was obviously at peace. That made my job a joy to do as I knew there was no more suffering for her and she was at peace with everything. I felt very honoured to be doing the final care for her.

The next morning everyone was upset about her death and kept asking how I was. I really wasn't sure how I felt. I was still numb, but felt okay because I knew she wasn't suffering. When I left the ward it felt very surreal. For me, the saddest part was I never got to see her husband again. He was so grief stricken at losing her he went back to Africa. He was a military man and the last I heard was he went back to the Army.

As a nurse we are always told not to get involved with patients, to stay emotionally free. Realistically, that is impossible. So when something like this does happen and you're not used to it, you cope by shoving it down, putting it aside and not thinking about it. Of course all the associated emotions won't stay buried forever, so over the years I have had to face the grief I had around that night and let go of it. Many times I have asked, "Why me? Why on my last night?" In reality she felt safe to go, it was her time to go and I was able to be there to help her and for I will always feel privileged. Her smile and peacefulness that night gave me back a sense of faith that there was more out there, that maybe, just maybe, there was a God. She helped me start to think about things differently. She started to change my viewpoint without even being there in the physical sense.

I still think of her to this day and at times I still get tearful at the memories. But with the tears there is always a smile, a smile I hope to reflect hers the night she died. All nurses have patients they care for who, for whatever reason, they never forget. She is one of mine. She will always be with me wherever I go and I know that is okay. She is one of my angels.

To add to this story, after nineteen years she came to me as one of my guides when four of us were at the river to do a ceremonial dance. We were connecting with the ways of old, clearing away energies for ourselves and for women across the world, it was amazing. I felt like I was dancing for women all over the world who weren't able to join us: those who were caught up in war and those who were condemned for just being women. I was dancing for them all as well as for me. It felt very liberating as we reconnected with our roots and to the goddess we each have within. As we danced we connected back with how it used to be when women were respected and acknowledged for their wisdom, comradeship and their nurturing and loving ways. A few days after the ceremony I wrote about it and right at the end of the account it suddenly hit me that the energy I had felt as we danced was in fact a person, my patient from nineteen years ago. I realised she had just shown me she was indeed one of my angels, which set off a flood of tears in me.

The second patient I would like to talk about is a little girl called Sophie. This is her real name as I have permission from her mum and dad to use it. Over the months, while she received treatment, she became one of our regular patients. As always you try not to have favourites as all patients are special, but somehow the odd one catches you unaware. Working in the Children's Ward I can't imagine what each child and parent go through during their time with us. I have a lot of compassion for them because not only are the children special, but the parents are too as they have to deal with all the emotional turmoil that goes with having a sick child.

Sophie was diagnosed at twelve months old with a rare form of cancer and, sadly, all treatment given to her did not work. The last hope was a bone marrow transplant, but again, sadly, that also failed and Sophie was sent home to die. I remember the first time I saw her when she came back from Christchurch after her treatment. She did not look like the Sophie we knew at all. I burst into tears after I left the room as it was really hard to see her like that. Sophie was sent home with twenty-four hour care. I was working a night shift on the ward, when I was asked if I could care for Sophie that night in her home. As I got to the front door and went into the house, I still had a feeling something wasn't right. On returning from Christchurch Sophie had been given at least two to three weeks to live, but when I walked in that night I knew something was wrong. Her mum hadn't been sleeping and had just taken a sleeping tablet. Sophie was in her room hooked up to a drip for fluids. I sat with her and read to her and sent her loving healing. What happened next is that Sophie started to bleed just a tiny little bit from the nose, which can be a sign that a person is nearing the end. I continued to sit with her for a little bit, as I knew her mum needed sleep.

However, it happened again and this time there was a bit more blood. This prompted me to take action. She told me (through her spirit) she wanted to be with her mum and dad in the living room. What you need to understand is that back in those days I wasn't sure about any of this "stuff"—healing and spiritual things were all new to me and I questioned it a lot! But it was clear what she wanted, and, with the physical signs she had shown me, I thought she didn't have long left at all. So I made the decision to wake up her mum and dad and tell them. Of course they were a bit dazed and confused, but we all went into the living room. To be able to move Sophie I first had to disconnect her drip, an act I questioned as I knew it wouldn't be an easy task to reconnect it. But I trusted what Sophie had shown me. As we all sat in the living room Sophie was happy because she was with both her parents and could hear them talk about her. I knew she was okay. Of course, I still doubted myself, but I followed Sophie's lead. At about five in the morning her dad went to bed for a while, which just left her mum, Sophie and me. But really this was a moment for Sophie and her mum. Towards the end of that night you could see Sophie was deteriorating so I went and woke her dad

Her mum asked me to give her a little pain relief as she believed changing the nappy would be painful for Sophie. Together we changed her nappy, then as her mum picked her up, Sophie said goodbye to her mum and gave her last breath. As she was being cuddled she passed away in her mum's arms. I don't want to go into details about her actual passing, but to suffice to say, she definitely knew her parents were there and the love that surrounded her helped her to pass away peacefully.

94

Afterwards, I drove home in shock. It was just as well the car knew its way as I certainly wasn't concentrating too much on the road that morning. Like the previous story, I didn't know how to process the grief I experienced as a result of Sophie's passing. It's hard to keep a balance between being a professional, while at the same time feeling the pain of grief because someone in your care has died. What do you do? How do you react? This is one thing you are not taught when you train to be a nurse, but I guess something like that can't be taught as it is so personal and individual and everyone reacts differently. I was in shock and numb for quite a while after Sophie died. I was trying to process what had happened that night and what she had shown me. I found myself wondering about how the parents were and how they felt her final hours had been. For a long time all these thought kept going around my head and there were times when I felt I wasn't handling things as well as I might.

In the time after her death, I kept in touch with Sophie's parents, and during one visit her mum gave me two photographs of Sophie, which I still treasure. Over the years I have also made contact with the parents on several occasions. Once, sometime after her death, Sophie contacted me and asked me to ring her mum, which I did. I was a little nervous as it had been some time since we had spoken and I didn't know what I was going to say, or how the call would go. In the end I just spoke the truth. It turned out that phone call had come at a very important time in the mum's life.

One night I had just gone to bed and some words kept coming into my head. I had to get out of my bed and write them down. I ended up writing a poem for

Sophie's parents; the words came from Sophie and I just wrote them down on her behalf. That was on the tenth anniversary of her death.

Then, eleven years later, I caught up with the mum for a coffee. Our meeting had been a long time coming but we easily talked about Sophie and other things. Driving back into town I was suddenly overcome by the same feelings I had experienced the morning Sophie had passed away. I suddenly realised I was driving the exact same route I had driven the morning of Sophie's death, but it was now eleven years later. I had huge pain in my shoulder and realised it was pain I had held onto for Sophie. Lots were beginning to make sense with regard to the pain we do hold onto in our body. I was also beginning to understand that when we face the pain, we can finally release it. As I continued home I felt at peace as I knew I had let a lot go.

I think a lot about Sophie and she certainly pops in to say hello, which I think is great. She has taught me a lot about compassion and through her I have realized it is okay to feel grief. However, she has taught me so much more. She showed me that night she knew what was happening to her. She knew it was her time to go. I know this will sound unrealistic to some people, but trust me she did. How she communicated with me that night was not in the usual way we use to communicate with each other (although we are all capable of doing this) but communicate she did as I was very thankful I was able to assist her.

I will always remember her dad saying he had often worried that when Sophie's time came, whether he should phone people in the middle of the night or wait until the morning. Well Sophie solved that dilemma for him as she passed away a few minutes before seven in the morning. You see, she knew and had always been communicating with us, and she still is.

I thank Sophie from the bottom of my heart, as with the story before, both people have brought me much insight and if it had not been for them I do not think I would be where I am at this time in my learning. I feel very rich as a result of their teachings. However, I still feel deeply for the parents, husband and families who lost these two people as I know they both touched and enriched the hearts of those closest to them and their loss is still very much felt today. I honour each and everyone one of them for the journey they are on, and I thank them for allowing me to be a small part of that. I can still feel their grief, and if I could wave a magic wand to make it better, I would. To them both, you are angels.

**In memory of Sophie**

**Ten years have gone by**

Sophie is my name
And playing was my game
I laughed, giggled and grinned so much

To my wonderful mum, I thank you
For the cuddles, kisses and love you gave
But I feel your pain

To my hearty dad, don't be sad
You were a wonderful dad
But I feel your pain

The night that came
I truly had no pain
I took a sigh
And said a long goodbye

Close your eyes, go within
For you will see me there
Close your mind, open your heart, go within
For you will feel me there

Have no fear
Have only hope
For I truly am a float

It's a wonderful thing
What you believe in
Believe in me, believe in you
And it shall be

## Chapter Eight
## My brother saved my life

*Miracles happen every day if we have our eyes and ears open to see and hear them.*

Do you believe in angels? Sometimes I don't think people know how to answer that question if they are asked. Many people wouldn't dare to say they believe in something that can't be seen and others may ridicule. Do I believe in angels? Now I can categorically answer, "Yes," to that question. Reflecting back on some of the experiences I have had, and knowing a little bit more now about the bigger picture of life, I feel certain when I say, "Yes, no questions asked." As a child I am sure I did believe in angels and all sorts of things. However, as a young adult I was probably too busy questioning everything and not believing in anything, part of me so wanted to, but the other part thought it was impossible.

One night when I was fifteen and at boarding school in Britain, we were all getting ready for bed as usual. The lights had just gone out when suddenly I felt the sheets at the bottom of my bed go down, just ever so slightly, like someone had placed the palm of their hand on the bed. I froze thinking, "What on earth was that?" I knew no one had snuck up as every floorboard in the corridor leading to the room creaked with each step. No one, and I mean no one, could have walked along that corridor without making a creak or two! I must have lay there frozen for at least twenty minutes before I brave enough to move and see if anything or anyone was there. Of course not a single soul was to be seen. It was ages before I could get to sleep as I couldn't figure out what had happened. It took me a few days before I asked the other girls if they had any similar experiences happen to them and they said, "No." Sometime later I found out the priest who used to live in that house had died and he quite often checked on the girls at night. That must be it I thought, somehow I felt the sheets go down when he must have touched them. I never told too many people that story, just the girls I shared the room with.

That was my first recollection of strange things happening. The second was after my brother's life support machine had been switched off. We had all gone into his hospital room and said our goodbyes before they stopped the machine and removed all the tubing. We were told it would take about fifteen minutes before we were allowed back in to see him once they had cleaned him up a bit. There were six of us in the waiting room. I was sitting with my back to the wall, looking towards the door. Suddenly I saw my brother standing at the doorway. He was dressed in the clothes I had last seen him in and he had his wig and glasses on; it was definitely him. I just kept looking from him to the door and to the others in the room, as if to say, "Can you see him too?" It was obvious they couldn't, so I just sat there and we started to talk, not out loud, just in my head. He was telling me about all the things he had wanted but hadn't because he knew mum would have disapproved because of his illness. We were both just laughing at this. He was listening closely to everything that was being said in that waiting room. I kept shaking my head and closing my eyes and opening them again to see if he was still there; he was. I kept thinking I must be going crazy: "How can this be? He is clinically dead. How can I be seeing him?" But I was and it was real, it was as real as the hand at the end of my arm. I found the experience to be comforting; I was talking to my brother and thought "This is okay." Just before a nurse then came to tell us we could go in and see him, he disappeared from the waiting room as quickly as he appeared. When I went into his room and looked at his body lying there, after the experience I had just had I knew that the person who was lying on that bed was not my brother, it was just a shell, there was no one in there anymore. What I had seen minutes before was real and had been my brother.

At that moment I just lost it and ran out of the Intensive Care Unit, I ran down the corridor, to where I had no idea, I just kept running. I have no idea how long I stayed away or where I ended up. I'm not sure if I went back to the unit or if I met everyone outside, I can't really recall. The next thing I do remember is standing outside the hospital and mum saying she wasn't sure if he wanted to be buried or cremated she was worried about it. I think it might have been of his friends who had said cremated, but I'm not really sure, someone did know though which was important. Mum wasn't too happy with that as she wanted a grave where she could visit him. To keep everyone happy, he was cremated and his ashes were put in the graveyard with a head stone. As we stood outside the hospital Christmas carols were being sung and at the very moment we left the hospital Silent Night was being sung. Every time I hear that carol it always take me back to that moment in time. Then, about two years ago, I actually listened to the words properly and was when the words "sleep in heavenly peace" came up, well, that was it, I just burst out into tears. I knew then the words of the carol had been a sign the night we left the hospital, but it had taken me to really listen to the words to realise he was finally at peace.

He died nineteen years ago. It has been nineteen years since I came to New Zealand. When I was coming over I had to have a return ticket even though I didn't want one, I had to have one. So I randomly booked my return flight for December, thinking, "I'll never use it." However, I received the call from my mum on the 7th December telling me my brother had been taken ill and was in Intensive Care. My return ticket, the one I never expected to use, was booked for the tenth or eleventh and that was the ticket I used to go back. Random? Coincidence? Who knows, but for the fact I had the ticket months before and never thought I would use, shows me there is a lot more to life than what we realise. My brother died on the nineteenth of December and we buried him on the twenty-second; needless to say Christmas is never easy. You never forget things like that, but time does make it a little easier to bear. I remember sitting in the living room on Christmas Day thinking he would walk through the door in a minute and it had all been a bad dream. But he never did walk through the door and it wasn't a dream. I have no idea how we got through Christmas that year, but we did.

I returned to New Zealand on New Year's Eve. Normally, every time I returned to wherever I was living, I felt guilty leaving everyone behind. Strangely, this time, I didn't. I had just buried my brother and I was going back to New Zealand and I didn't feel guilty. I couldn't figure that out. For me it feels that when he died he saved my life in so many ways I never believed possible.

By seeing him and talking with him in the waiting room he showed me actually there was a lot more out there and my job was to start looking, which I did, but it wasn't easy and it took time for me to warm to the idea. It's only in hindsight I can see how he helped to change my life, after all that was nineteen years ago and I'm in a completely different space now to where I was back then.

My brother had been unwell since he was six months of age with a condition called Autoimmune Deficiency Syndrome, not a lot is known about. From what I can understand, both my parents have a defective gene that, when they produced a son, came out in him. My other brother is also affected by the same condition, but he has a milder version. For years I tried to understand the condition and worried I was a carrier. It wasn't until I fell pregnant I managed to get it explained to me properly that both partners had to have the affected gene for it to be passed on to their children. So, I was okay. I can't tell you what a relief that was. In my brother it caused his immune system and glands not to work and over time they started shutting down. When he was younger, his body wasn't able to produce calcium. His nails were always humped, never flat, and he had thrush constantly. He spent most of his youth in and out of hospital. Then he was diagnosed with diabetes, which really started to fight the body. At thirteen, he developed Alopecia (loss of hair) and he never had a normal bowel motion. He was also diagnosed with Addison's disease when he was young. Trying to sort out his medical problems was a nightmare. Each time one was sorted it would have a counter effect on one of his other problems and so it went on. It was a roller coaster of a ride trying to get him sorted. Throughout it all he always kept his sense of humour. Very rarely did people ever see him having a bad day, which of course he did, but he just got on with it. Towards the end everything was getting quite hard for him. He couldn't eat oranges as they would interfere with one of his drugs and he was really struggling to cope with having so many things he could and couldn't do as a result of his many conditions; it was really getting to him. He had many close calls, and, bit by bit, his body was shutting down.

He used to wear a wig. One day he was going to an appointment at the hospital when there was a huge gust of wind literally took his hair off his head; his wig went flying to the nearest tree. Of course, we were in stitches and laughed and laughed at his expense. But he didn't see the funny side of it and, I guess, why would he? It was even funnier when he explained how he had to go and retrieve the wig from the tree. He did give us a good laugh that day. Later on, when telling the story, he could laugh about it. He was, however, always very serious and didn't laugh a great deal around us, but I think it was a different story when he was with his friends. Even as a child he never used to smile a lot. I always remember mum trying to make him laugh, or saying things like, "Smile if you like" and he would give a small smirk but not much else.

Then, not long before he died, he went on a live chat show. I was working in London at the time and so made sure some of the patients on my ward had the TV on the right channel so I could watch. No one ever saw him without his wig; at home was the only place where he would take it off. One day he decided that, if he was going to take his wig off, rather than doing it over and over for many different people, he thought the easiest solution was just to do it on TV for everyone to see. So that's what he did. The focus of the show was hair loss in men and my brother was one of the people they had invited on to the show to talk about it. At the end of his segment he took off his wig for all to see; this was huge for him and I felt very proud of him for his courage.

The night he was taken ill was his third scare. He had had two other close calls but had pulled through them. This night he was in his room; mum's room was opposite. Both rooms had a phone, so he phoned mum in her room to tell her he wasn't feeling well. She immediately called the ambulance and by the time it got there he was going into heart failure. In the back of the ambulance he arrested; his heart stopped beating so they spent quite a while trying to resuscitate him. Eventually, they set off to the hospital, but it wasn't looking good. He had been in Intensive Care for a few days when they did a brain scan to see what was happening. Sadly, we were told there was no brain activity. Those are the hardest words you can hear. When I heard them, I kept thinking, "No! You have it wrong. Do another test. That can't be the case, do another test." Even though I work in the profession, and I knew the results were based on a few tests, when it's personal you lose all logic and common sense and believe they must be wrong, that's not right; so many thoughts run through your head. However, I eventually came to accept there was nothing that could be done for him.

One of the hardest parts about death is having to tell everyone, that is not an easy task. I remember I had to ring a good family friend and she was devastated and she kept referring to my brother as her "wee boy;" she always had a soft spot for him, which was great. Everyone was devastated, except the one person who you would expect:

my dad. By this time my parents were separated, so mum rang him with the news. I sat opposite her in the lounge while she was on the phone and I could hear what she was saying. Part way through the call she was starting to get really upset, which upset me. I was shouting at her, telling her to get off the phone because we didn't need his help. But she was trying to get the funeral sorted and was asking for his help to pay for things. He refused to help and even said he wasn't his son! What can you say to that? Even at a time like this my dad still refused to take any responsibility and do the right thing. It was the Army that stepped in and helped mum with the arrangements, not my dad.

At the funeral I intended to absolutely blast into him, and I mean blast. I was furious, but mum kept saying she didn't want any trouble, and, of course, she was starting to get upset. So, for that reason and only that reason, I did not say anything to him. You may think refusing to pay for part of his son's funeral was bad enough, but it didn't stop there. He was forced to attend by his mum and his sister. They sat on either side of him in the car on the way to the church to make sure he got there. At the church, he stood at the back for the whole service and, as soon as it was finished, he left before anyone could see him, say anything, or do anything. An older gentleman who worked with my brother in the club attended the funeral. He was devastated and was in tears. He told my father how sorry he was about dad's loss. Dad just walked straight passed him without a word or a "thank you," being said. I watched the back of him as he walked away. I had never felt so much rage and contempt for another person as I did at that moment, and that was the person I had to call my dad.

I was livid, ropeable and so, so angry at his behaviour; and I felt cheated I hadn't been allowed to say anything to him for fear of upsetting mum too much. So these feelings probably festered away in me for years. From time to time, I would talk about it and still be angry, which wasn't a good place to be in. Even now, as I write about it for the first time, I can still feel some anger about the fact a father would say and do such things to his own son. Just for the record my mother did not sleep with anyone other than my father, so there is no question he was the father. I never thought anyone could stoop so low, but I was wrong, as it was proven to me that day just how low a person can go.

I hadn't spoken to my father in years, and then, a few years ago, I got a call from mum saying dad had died. Apparently he had cancer of either the liver or bowel, I can't quite remember. He had been on holiday in the Caribbean with his new lady friend, who we were later told looked surprisingly like mum, when he had taken a turn for the worse and came back home. We were told of his death a few days after the funeral. I remember lying in bed early one morning after I heard. I had a few tears and that was it. I had done so much inner work on my dad and I think I had dealt with it all; I had nothing left for this man. To me, that is really sad and it should never be like that, but in my case it was. He may have been my biological father, but that was where it stops. Writing all this down now, about the funeral and what my dad did, is quite cathartic and it has allowed me to see how sad and childlike a person he actually was. I don't think he ever grew up and became an adult, in the real sense. I think he always wanted people to take care of him so he didn't have to have the responsibility of doing it for himself. And he certainly never took responsibility for his own actions, never. I thought I still had anger there around the funeral but in writing this I know I don't; I have worked through it all, thank goodness. Of course there will still be times when it will come back, but for the majority, I have dealt with it. In his passing he will have to deal with all the things he never did, and, who knows, maybe his life journey was to treat his children in a horrendous way so they could learn forgiveness and humility. I don't know, but I know there has to be a bigger plan for all of this, as life doesn't present so much suffering and pain just for the sake of it. I don't know what he signed up for before he was born, but I do know it would have been something. When you realise there is a bigger picture, a bigger plan, it is difficult to stay angry or mad; what's the point, it is only you that is suffering, no one else. When you can see life through different glasses by removing the element of emotion, things start to make a little more sense. It's the emotions that cloud us as we get so caught up in them, but they are there to guide us, not for us to become them. Emotions show us when something isn't right and it is our job to deal with them and let them go. But we hold onto them as if they belong to us, but they don't.

The next big question is, where does karma fit into all of this? The families we choose to be born into have probably been with us for many lifetimes, except we may have been the parent, grandparent or child in different generations. So how does that idea fit with this life? I remember reading Sue Nicholson's book *A call from the Other Side*. This is her life story. When her mum was dying she saw that, in a previous lifetime, she had been the mum and her mother had been the daughter. She could see how her mother had been as a daughter and this insight had opened her eyes and given her a different understanding of her mother. This is an example of learning from previous mistakes and trying to stop that cycle from going on. I'd like to think we can all stop the cycles in our lives that are damaging, but first we have to become aware of it in order to stop it. We need to be aware of what belief patterns have been bestowed upon us from both our family of today and our ancestral ones through the generations. By developing awareness we can stop the cycle of unhealthy values in our lives.

Love is what it should all be about, but, most of the times, we think love is something other people give to us. Sadly, many of us have forgotten the one and only person who really should be giving us love are ourselves. We get so busy doing for others and putting others first that we put ourselves last. We are at the bottom of the heap when, in fact, we should be at the top. If we love ourselves first then all else fits into place and, most importantly, we will be happy and won't need love from other people, although if it happens the love we share with another person will be healthier than it would be if we didn't love ourselves first.

There are different thoughts on karma "you get back what you have sown, tenfold," true or not I don't really know at this stage. All I do know and believe is we can change our circumstances through the choices we make; hence we can break the karma chain, if that is what it is about.

Death is never easy to deal with, especially when it is someone you love who passes. I had always feared this day happening and, while I knew it would come, I could never have been fully prepared, no matter what I thought. My brother was the only person in my family who would ever come and visit me wherever I was living; I am sure New Zealand would have been next on his list to visit me. I was amazed at how many people he had touched in his short life; he was twenty nine when he died.

Sadly, time ran out for him, but he is certainly here in spirit. Just because a person is no longer in this physical world, in a physical body does not mean that they are lost to us. It's just we can't see them, (some can of course) but they are very much present in spirit. Maybe one day our views on death may change and we will be able to cope with death a lot better than what we do at the moment.

Hindsight is wonderful and I can look back now and be thankful for the experience my brother's death has given and continues to give me. When it happened I wouldn't have been able to say that, and to be honest, at the time I would never have believed I would be saying it now either. I give thanks because it was his death, along with the other two experiences I had with the patients mentioned in the previous chapter, which saved me. Again, it is only with hindsight I can see that now. Each one of these people looked peaceful and serene in death, and talking to my brother in the waiting room as they were switching his life support off showed me there is life after death.

For a long time I puzzled over what happened with my brother and it was only a couple of years ago I managed to figure it out. When they were switching off his life support, his soul left his body. Appearing in the waiting room was his way of showing me that even in death he was okay. I now understand why I couldn't cope when I saw his physical body lying on the bed. I had just seen my brother, not the shell that was left.

I once had a spiritual reading in which my brother came through. This time it was his turn to be on his high horse, and tell me about a few things I needed to do. Normally, when he had been alive, it had been the other way round, with me telling him what to do. I just laughed at this and thought, "How ironic."

This next little story I have permission from my client to share, though I still won't use names. When she was pregnant for the first time she had a miscarriage. As you can imagine, that experience was devastating. Although she went on to have more children who were all healthy and well, her first child was never far from her mind. At this time she didn't know what sex it was, and didn't have a name for the child. The first time she came to see me her child was very present and showed me it wanted to be a part of her life. We found it was indeed a boy and, later on, she was able to name him with the other family members. In another session I was told her son was not dead and he wanted to be a part of her family. Slowly it dawned on me what I was being told. Just because we see people as being dead physically, they are not dead in their own eyes; rather they are still alive in a spiritual sense. There is nothing tangible to touch, and we do all have the ability to see spirit if we are open to that possibility. As I continued to work with this lady, it became clear her son was there with them and wanted to be a part of the family, just not in the physical sense. That of course made sense and got me thinking it would be great if we could all view the death of loved ones, and our experience of their deaths, in that way. We could still have them involved in our lives, instead of our allowing our bodies to be consumed by grief; which is of no help to anyone, let alone those who have died. Slowly the grief this lady held onto began to ease and she started to feel at peace with what had happened. Sometime later, my client held a birthday party for her first born son who, for whatever reason, had chosen to be part of her life as spirit rather than in the physical world. How absolutely amazing I thought, what a great way to celebrate all forms of life, living or not.

# Chapter Nine
## The deep layer of the onion revealed

*Look through the eyes of a child and you will see*
*innocence, fun and laughter.*
*If that innocence isn't there how do the eyes look then?*

When I returned to New Zealand after my brother's death, I stayed in Auckland for a few months but soon decided it was time to move and go elsewhere. I opted to head to the South Island, Queenstown to be exact. Everyone thought I was mad and believed I would be back in Auckland before long. Without taking their views seriously, I packed up my car and headed off. I took about a week to get there, finding my flatmates on the journey. When I arrived in Queenstown I had no job, but was sure I would get a nursing job as I had always managed to find something in this line of work before. However, this time it was not to be, so I accepted work in a café. That was a challenge: hard work for very little money. I tried to last as long as I could in Queenstown and kept saying to myself that things will get better. Eventually, however, I had to call it quits, pack up the car and leave town. I had managed to stay for a month before the money had run out. After I filled the car with petrol on the way out of town, I had five dollars left in my purse. I headed to Dunedin where I was able to stay with a good friend's parents until I got myself a job. This time I got a job working in the Paediatric Ward: I stayed there for three years.

At the end of the first year of Psychosynthesis I had peeled away many, many layers of the onion I talk about, each time going deeper and deeper into my inner self. One Sunday morning I hit the big one. I was just relaxing in bed when suddenly I had these images of being in another bed when I was a child. I was petrified and I couldn't move; I literally couldn't move. I kept thinking and felt something had happened to me when I was a child. The image was in black and white and was like a horror movie that was happening to me and no one else. Over and over again I just kept seeing the same thing and each time I was unable to move. I froze; I can't remember for how long but I know it felt like it was hours, even the whole day.

As the scene repeated I knew I had been sexually abused by my dad when I was a little girl. As I came to this realisation, my God, I froze and couldn't move and remained like that for the rest of the day. I just lay on the bed in shock, not believing. I tried to convince myself this was someone else's story. It couldn't be mine, not me. I kept telling myself this over and over and over again. I kept thinking, "This is just a story. It's not real. It's not true." I didn't want to believe, couldn't believe, but the way my body was reacting I knew the truth. Deep down I had always known or had a feeling something wasn't right – a sixth sense, but could never put my finger on it until now when I was shown what it was. I was battling this knowledge, even though deep down I knew it was true, there was still a part of me that did not and could not believe the truth. "What do I do? Where do I go? How do I deal with this?" So many questions my head was spinning, my body was reeling, emotionally I felt sick to the stomach, and I was totally lost and alone. I had a whole raft of feelings I didn't know what to do. On the Monday I phoned Jay as I knew she was the only person at this time I could trust. I had quite a few sessions with her around the images and in each of those sessions it was confirmed I had been abused as a child by my dad.

After talking with Jay, I knew I had to tell someone about what had happened, but I was absolutely petrified they wouldn't believe me and would think I was making it up because of the way in which I had remembered. I also couldn't tell anyone until I had spoken to my mum first. I felt it wasn't fair or true to tell people in New Zealand before speaking to mum about it. That was the hardest phone call I have ever had to make. We had never really talked about things as a family, so for me to ring and say, "Oh, by the way, I've just remembered dad abused me as a child," was a very big deal. I was expecting her to turn around and say it was rubbish, but she never did. She told me she had asked when I was eighteen year old if dad had ever done anything to me, and at the time I had said, "No." She was curious as to why I was saying now, but I explained I had just remembered what had happened. I went on to say I wasn't too sure how old I had been, but I knew it was when I was quite young. Then she told me when I was four she would go out to work in a biscuit factory at night. We would be all ready for bed when she left; all dad had to do was put us to bed. As soon as she said that, I remembered how I had never wanted her to leave at night, I always wanted her to stay, but she never did; she had to go to work. We spoke for about two hours, and in many ways I felt relieved I had told her. I was also relieved she believed me, but I was still in shock from the fact it was true, this was real and it really did happen. Boy, did I feel sick, sick to my stomach.

Dad had a reputation for the ladies and was always playing away from home, even though mum never found this out until much later in their marriage. We had even sent him money to him when he was meant to have been away on a course but, instead, he was shacked up with another woman. One time, while he was dancing with the daughter of one of his friends, and with everyone around to see, he tried to stick his tongue into her mouth. He also had a sexual harassment case brought against him by two women when he was a Housing Officer, but nothing happened as they later dropped the complaint. He left the Army not long after that. His departure was a little before his time. Was he pushed or encouraged to leave? We will never know.

I had kept the memory of this time dormant for thirty-two years. It is difficult for others to imagine what it is like to have something like this festering away inside, knowing all the time something wasn't quite right with you, but not knowing what. There were times when I thought it was all in my imagination. Then I rediscovered the truth, and was not prepared for the impact that knowledge would have on my life. I was at a loss to explain how I could have kept it quiet for so long. I wondered how on earth I did not remember. I also puzzled over how, for years, I thought my dad was the only one who loved me, that he was okay. I guess, in his own warped way, he did love me. He kept saying to me, "You're special. This is our secret" and, because it was dad who was telling me this, I believed it and I trusted him and I never told anyone. What used to also puzzle me was that whenever I was in bed, if I heard dad come up the stairs I would freeze in bed until I knew he was gone. If we were ever out and he wanted to hold or touch me I would always freeze yet again, and hate him touching me. I knew this was an unusual reaction but I could never figure out why, until now of course. I never knew why, I hated having to dance with him on those occasions we were out and he had been drinking. I had always put it down to the fact I didn't like his drinking. This is true, but there of course was a more sinister reason. So when all this came to light of what had happened when I was a child, all those thoughts came back to me, now they made total sense.

Looking back now, and knowing what I do, my inner child would have left my body during that time for that experience was too horrific to stay around for. It took a lot of work and a very long time for my inner child to come back into my body. For a long time she was absolutely scared and petrified. Who can blame her?

As mentioned back in Chapter Six, I have done a lot of work with my inner child. For a time she was hidden in a cave with lots of other children. When she returned to me I could only see the top half of her; the lower half just wasn't there. This makes sense now in light of what happened to me. When we have horrendous experiences, to help us cope with them, our spirit generally leaves our body until it is safe for it to come back in.

When I remembered what had happened to me, I guess I just dealt with what I had to, in a manner of speaking. There wasn't any emotion involved at this time, probably because I didn't want to believe it, and also because I wasn't able or equipped to emotionally cope with anything like this. All of my life things had been swept under the carpet, never to be mentioned or discussed. So I learnt early in life that if you don't show emotion or acknowledge things by talking about them, then everything will be fine; "all is well," so to speak. But all was not well.

I was numb for quite a while after this discovery, and found myself easily distracted. I had an old boyfriend who I had held onto for years and we were back in communication. I also had a new job in management and that was taking up a lot of my time. So you can see there were a few big issues I had to deal with at that time, which meant I really didn't have time for releasing any emotions around what I had remembered. It's only been through time I have been able to release a lot of the emotion associated with the abuse. In doing this I worked through many emotions and anger was one of the last to show its head. I hadn't thought I was holding onto anger. It probably sounds a bit strange I didn't think I had any anger, but that was truly what I believed. I am now grateful for the lack of anger because I think anger would have sent me over the edge. Anger wasn't an emotion I was used to, so I don't think I would have been able to cope with its intensity at that time. Instead, I experienced numbness, shock and disbelief, and, as I worked my way through each of these, over a period of time I did start to get angry.

I also had a physical reaction to what had happened. I was not able to eat properly as every time I did I would vomit. My bowels played havoc as well and I didn't have a normal bowel motion for months on end. I lost a lot of weight and people were worried, as they weren't sure what was happening. But I knew; I just couldn't tell. All this was happening at the same time as my new job. After I finished writing this I went to get some wood for the fire. As I was at the woodpile I started to wonder why everything happened that way. And for the first time I was able to see the underlying reason. The new job and getting back in touch with an old boyfriend were distractions from the truth and reality of what was happening for me at that time. I had to carry on doing what I doing and the distractions allowed me to do that. Even though my body was falling apart, I was still able to function in the day to day world. I now know I wasn't meant to fall apart at that time; that was to happen in stages, not all at once. The next part of my healing around this was to do with my partner-to-be and my daughter, but I didn't know it then. My healing at this time was also to do with being honest with myself at last. I had to face up to things I thought might happen, but probably won't, or that things did happen but I had forgotten about them. Now was the time to let them come to the surface so I could begin to heal by being truthful to myself.

So my old boyfriend came and went: I realised, finally, he wasn't for me. The new job in management came and went: I quickly discovered I was just the meat in the sandwich and the higher bosses had their own agenda; you rocked the boat and didn't fit in if you didn't agree with them. I learnt that even if you have the best intentions to make things better, it doesn't matter what you think or say, the powers that be will never listen. They may go through the motions of pretending to, but their attention is false. So I realised management wasn't where I wanted to be after all. I could waste all my time and energy getting nowhere, which I knew would end up with me getting more frustrated with the system.

Thankfully, I was covering for a woman who was on maternity leave for a year, so that was my out. At first part of me did think it might have been good to continue, but realistically, I would have got way too frustrated with the system. Little did I know that high levels of frustration were still to come, but that would be much later. For now I was shedding my old skin, old hurts and making way for the new. Remembering about the abuse was all part of that shift. Of course, at the time, I just didn't see it for what it was. In fact, it has taken me eleven years to actually perceive the change that occurred at that time. I know now there is a much bigger picture of what happens to us; we just don't comprehend it all at the time. In hindsight I am grateful for way it all happened, but I certainly wasn't grateful when it was all happening because I didn't really understand it all.

I asked myself the question, "how did I ever form relationships with people," more to the point "how was I able to have sexual relationships, with what had happened" I asked this for quite a long time before I finally got my answer. In having sexual relationships that was my way of obtaining and receiving affection. That was the only way I knew how, to have sex with someone was how you got attention and affection. I can't say love as that wasn't there; it was just means to an end. I was desperately trying to find love, but in all the wrong places and all the wrong way. None of my relationships ever lasted, ever, and not surprising is it when you see what happened. That is until I met Lyndsay and had my daughter, now I was ready. Up until then I certainly wasn't, of course I never knew any of this until looking back in hindsight seeing and being shown what it was all about.

Living with the realisation you have been abused by one of the people who were meant to be protecting you is huge. Over time I have had to deal with different ways in which the experience would raise its head in my life. One of the things I found most difficult was being able to trust people. Part of living with the knowledge you have been abused is you think others will abuse too. This of course is not true, but those thoughts slowly creep in and have a tendency of taking over, if allowed. When I look back at everything and everyone in my life, this experience has been a big part of what has moulded me. Each new experience I have will potentially bring up different issues for me that still need to be resolved. This has happened a few times and thankfully I was able to go inside and deal with whatever was coming up and let it go. If I hadn't done the work I had prior to discovering about the abuse, I really don't think I would have been able to deal with the thoughts in the way I did. Rather, I would have blamed, accused and who knows what else – all absolutely unrealistic responses, but natural for what had occurred. Luckily, I had enough knowledge to know I had to go deep inside of me to find the real answer and move forward. As I have said many a time before, "When we are ready to deal with it, there is a time and a place for everything to come out." Now, I guess, was the time for this knowledge to come to light. I was ready.

I have lived with what I called paranoia for a long time; paranoid that people were talking about me. Well, for the most part, they were, and it wasn't always nice either. I often overheard friends and relations talking about me. Sometimes I just had a feeling they were talking about me, and, if I confronted them they would always deny it. For the most part, however, that wasn't true as I had heard them. This has been huge for me: living my life in fear others are talking about me.

Not having a solid grounding in being loved, and knowing you were not loved also had a part to play. You try and not let the fact you were not loved bother you but it does. You try and say, "Well that's okay, that's their opinion." but not being valued matters hugely. It just feeds the thoughts that you are useless and worthless makes them bigger. So you shove the feelings down inside you and try and ignore them the best you can. Occasionally, however, they will raise their ugly head. When this happens I try to cope with it the best I can. Coping generally meant I would get quite low, not talk much, go into my shell and hide. I would then carry on as if I wasn't bothered, but I was, always.

One time I was at a friend's for Christmas. When she came in from night shift I heard her say to her mother that she wished she hadn't invited me to stay. Her mother reminded her she had in fact invited me so she should just get on with it and be polite. I lay in bed and froze. "Here we go again," I thought. She was a so called friend but here she is wishing I wasn't around. My immediate reaction was to run, but unfortunately I was stuck; I couldn't go anywhere as it was Christmas Day, and I had no car. I decided I could either go into my shell even more, knowing she never really wanted me there, or I could put on a brave face and pretend everything was fine; I did the latter. As we opened our presents I was smiling and pretending everything was fine, when the whole time inside I knew it was a farce.

While on holiday with the same friend sometime later, I overheard her talking about me to a guy she had met.

This time I confronted her and asked her why she had been talking about me. She denied it, but I knew she had as I had heard her. Gradually, my trust for this person was slowly dwindling. It probably sounds quite petty to write about people who talked about me behind my back, but for me it was a big deal and still is. Some might say I only *thought* I heard people say that, or I *thought* they were talking about me. This is absolutely possible, but I also know that when you hear in black and white and as clear as day words spoken by others, you know, you just know when it is about you. Remember, this was back in the days before I had started any inner work on myself at all. This was how I used to live my life: in paranoia that people were talking about me. Now I know people gossip; we all talk about each other in terms of, "She did this...," or "He did that...," and then let it go by moving onto the next subject. But for me it was important to know people liked me, and by talking about me behind my back they were showing me they didn't and I was hurt by their words. I had no solid grounding in being safe and secure in my own skin, I guess I was flying by the seat of my pants as they say and didn't know any different. I had no trust in me, I had no self-love for me and if I didn't have any of that in myself how could I expect anyone else to?

It's not until you start to work on yourself that you see how different things in life can be, and how crazy things have been in your life. I remember I had been in New Zealand for about two years when some friends came over and were traveling around. I caught up with them when they were in the South Island. I was quite nervous about the meeting as it had been a while since I had seen them. One had been a good friend when I was living in Britain, but we had drifted apart. Another was a very good friend and it was her I was really going to catch up with. I didn't really know the other two in the group. Normally with a situation like this I would have been paranoid to the hilt. I would be worrying about what they might say or do. My way of coping was to always try and be three steps ahead so I had no surprises as I had already anticipated what might happen. On this occasion I remember not having any of those feelings as I stood in the hotel foyer waiting to meet them. I was completely calm, felt good and was not worried at all. I stood there thinking, "Is this really happening?" and kept pinching myself, just to make sure it really was me. After all here were four people, two I knew, two of them I didn't. Just that scenario would set alarm bells off in me, but it didn't this time. I felt amazingly okay and comfortable; feelings I hadn't had before in social situations. Everyone was meant to be coming to my place, but the plans changed and only two of us ended up going to my place. Again, I was absolutely fine with this; in fact it was perfect as she was the only person I really wanted to catch up with. Normally if plans changed like I would have sent myself crazy thinking, "They don't like me." "What have I done?" The list would have continued. This time, however, I was fine, in fact I was more than fine, it was the perfect solution for all.

It was at this moment when I realised all the work I had been doing on myself was working. I can't tell you how ecstatic I was, to know what I was doing was truly working. While standing in the foyer was also the first time I realised just how much I had been living my life constantly worrying about what people thought or said. Boy, to realise I lived my life like that was huge. I now understood living like that had taken so much energy from me and I understood why I felt really heavy. This sudden awareness was a big surprise and wakeup call as I realised just how much I had lived like that. By the same token it was good to have confirmation of how I was changing and changing for the better. I didn't know any different, this was how I lived my life. Seeing this change really opened my eyes for me. I was quite horrified, but when you are in the thick of it, you don't know any different. How can you change when you don't know what needs changing if that is what you have always done? My change was due to doing the Psychosynthesis sessions and of course Jay who had helped me to open up to the possibility of change.

The work we do on ourselves never stops, and since writing this I have had a further realisation relating to the state of what I have called paranoia. However, I can now actually see I am very much in tune with what people think say and do. I have always been able to feel their energy and sense when they didn't like me or could pick up on what they were thinking about me. By acknowledging I can pick up on others energies I now know what I called a state of paranoia back then is quite different. I have to deal with this information knowing that's it not just in my head and I'm not going crazy and never was, even though I always believed I was. There was a legitimate reason for all those feelings I had around it. It has taken me about fifteen years to see the truth of my interactions with others. We all get information on a need to know basis; it only comes through when we are ready to hear and see what we need to do. If I had been told earlier I could pick up on people's energy, I wouldn't have been able to understand it as I can at this moment in time. And of course I am sure there will be yet another element to this as there always is. The reality of what I understand today will change and deepen again in the

125

next few years as I continue doing my own inner work, after all, that is what it is all about and nothing is set in stone.

# Chapter Ten
# Impact of emotions

*Expect the unexpected and all can change and be quite magical.*

When writing your own story you think it's a breeze as it's about you, and all the information is at your fingertips! However, in reality, it's not as easy as that. Each time I start to write about what I call the "hard emotional stuff" I stop, but I stop without really realizing why. It has been quite a few months since I wrote Chapter Nine and of course, at the time, I never actually paid much attention to the words that appeared on the page. Today I was re-reading some of the chapters to see where I was at and as I read Chapter Nine it dawned on me why I had stopped writing, because of all the "hard emotional stuff." In the past few months three or four messages about my writing have come from friends and clients. They ask how the book is going and they have encouraged me to keep writing. "Yes, yes, I will." I say. The intention has been there but I have never actually sat down to write, until now. So here I am, back again after a few months off and I have to reassess and readjust emotionally with what I am writing about.

Emotions, don't we love them? Well, we do when everything goes our way and we feel good. We loathe or fear them when things don't go our way and a whole raft of inner demons is brought up in us, even some we probably never knew existed. I know over the years that this has certainly been the case with me. But shouldn't be a surprise though, because unless you are encouraged to express your emotions and be honest with them, where do we put the emotions inside of us. You may of course be a person who can let go of their emotions quite well, sometimes even with no regard for how others feelings. For example, you might feel good while you are ranting and raving and shouting, but what about the person on the receiving end, do they feel good? I very much doubt it. Either way we don't win with our emotions, do we? We run, we hide from our emotions, or we shove them down deep or expel them at a hundred miles an hour. These ways of dealing with emotions are damaging. What we do need to do is get a balance with them. We need to express them in a healthy way which is not damaging to anyone else or ourselves. We need to acknowledge them and work with them, rather than expel them at others. Yes, we do need to express our anger. However, most of the time it isn't the people we are angry at; it's whatever happened that has triggered the anger; that's the key point. It's not the person causing the emotion, rather the person is showing you something is not quite right inside of you and really they are just helping you. To realise this will allow us to work with emotions in a healthy non blaming way.

Through my work over the years, each time I have discussed emotions with clients guaranteed the words what I am saying, have also applied to me. One of my favourite sayings is "What we teach is what we need to learn the most." Through my work and in my life I have been shown over and over this is very true. So, as I am talking to my clients I start to get the alarm bells go off in my head. "Ah, I wonder is this relevant for me?" and of course it is. So you see my clients are also my teachers.

After many years of work I am now starting to feel a little bit more comfortable with the emotions I have. Rather than hide from them I recognize them, not always straight away I must add, as sometimes it can be after I have reacted to a crisis I then see the emotion for what it really is. But I am being more honest and open to them than I guess I ever have done in the past. Nothing happens quickly when you do your own inner work; it takes time. How I describe it to clients is that it's like working behind the scenes on a play, you see the actors but you don't see the people behind the scenes. You know they are there and without them the show wouldn't have happened, over time things get done and change slowly. That's how I describe doing inner work. It's very subtle because you don't see change at first, but you trust and know it is happening as you slowly see and feel the change in yourself. Basically the work is slow and ongoing, but the more you do the wiser and smarter you become at working with it all.

Now when I wonder where the emotion is coming from when I start to get angry or annoyed, I can meditate and find out exactly where it started and let it go. There are times, however, I don't do this as I'm too far gone in the emotion and I react to it rather than see it for what it is, a way of telling me something isn't right inside of me.

Jay once told to us to be aware of our feelings because they are our guides. She also warned us not to become our emotions. I understood be aware of them but not really the part about not becoming them. When you are upset, angry, jealous, whatever the emotion is it is hard not to become that emotion when you are in the thick of it. However, since I last wrote, I am beginning to see how important it really is not become the emotion. It's okay to feel it of course, but you must observe it by stepping back and saying, "I am not that emotion. I feel it but I will not become it." As soon as you become an emotion you are entrenched in it and you can't see a logical solution. If, however, you step back and observe the emotion by saying, "Ah, that's interesting; why am I doing that?" Ask and watch what you are shown and you will clear an emotion more quickly by being aware of it and recognizing it. What I do now if I have a strong emotion come up, and I do trust me, is to go straight into meditation, find out what is happening and by the end of the meditation I have an answer and the emotion has dissolved itself, with no harm done to myself or any other innocent passer-by who may have received an earful of strong emotion I had not dealt with. It sounds simple; it is simple and best of all it works!

For years I had not been "present in my own body." I had first heard of this concept doing a session with Jay. I remember walking up a busy street one day and I could feel that, even though I was physically walking on the pavement, I could feel I was in fact elsewhere. I had never experienced it like that before. I was starting to understand what, "you're not in your body" meant. As mentioned in Chapter Nine, when horrendous things happen to us this is how our body deals with it. So what I was beginning to discover in my work is that a lot of my clients weren't present in their bodies either. Classic signs not being present can include feeling spacey, not able think straight, and possibly light headed. Of course these are symptoms for other conditions as well, but it could just be one of them is you are not in your body.

A great way for getting yourself back into your body is by doing what we call, grounding yourself. There are a few ways you can this. One of them is by eating more red meat, or you can use certain crystals to help ground you. The main one I use with clients is to imagine they are a tree. From under their feet they can see the roots of the tree grow into the ground. They use these roots to help keep them safely grounded on the ground! In other words the roots are holding their feet firmly on the ground and they are not going anywhere. This is a great one to use and I have used it many times not only on clients but also on myself. To help us release the tension that is held in our bodies from all the old emotional wounds we are holding on to, we must be present in our body, we must allow ourselves to feel our body, which in turns enables us to feel the emotion so we can then let it go out of our body. Our body no longer needs to hold onto it. But we can't really do that unless we are present in our body. We can, it's just it won't be as effective as to when we are in our body

We learn through feeling rather than thinking as thinking is too limiting. My new mantra at the moment for my clients is, "I need to feel my body, not think what's wrong with my body. I need to feel it." The only way babies can communicate with us is through crying, so we try to resolve their discomfort by picking them up and cuddling, feeding or changing them. The only way our body can communicate with us is by giving us pain. Then we know something is not right, but mainly we don't like pain because we see it as a hindrance that is stopping us from doing what we need to. "Give me some tablets to take the pain away so I can get on with what I am meant to be doing," we say and think to ourselves.

With a tablet the pain goes away. Great, but eventually it will come back, sometimes worse or we will get another type of pain and so the cycle keeps going. However, pain is our body's way of communicating with us. If we took a little bit of time to ask, "Why is my body doing this? What am I ignoring?" By asking these questions we would then know how to help our body by discovering where the pain is coming from. But most of us don't do this. We ignore pain and hope it will go away. I am now teaching my clients to look at pain as our friend not the enemy, as we generally like to see it as. The pain is there for a reason and if we stop, ask and listen we will find out what to do with it. Of course this will seem ridiculous and foreign to some, which is not surprising when you look at how we get brainwashed and bombarded with ideas on TV: soldier on, take this tablet for this, but then you need another to combat the side effect of the first one and so the cycle of ignoring what our bodies are trying to tell us just keeps going. Our bodies are so designed to help put systems out of balance back into balance, but that takes a little bit of time, something in this modern society we do not make allowance for: time to rest, to listen, to sleep, to be sick when we are sick. Of course at times we need to take tablets depending on what is happening for us, but what I am saying is we need to give our body time to simply try and sort itself out, rather than immediately reaching for a quick fix which will help us keep rushing round like headless chooks— doesn't make for a good sight does it?

Life is always about finding the balance between body, mind and spirit. Most of the time we are led by our mind, and have been for generations. Often that's why it can be hard to sit and meditate because our mind is used to being in charge and controlling us. When we meditate we go to our heart centre, which is a move away from our mind and our mind doesn't like that. But if you stop and listen to yourself for a minute and you would hear how much chatter goes on in your head: "This is sore, I should take a tablet" "Is it something serious?" "Do I need to go to the doctor?" "I don't have time to be sick" and the self-talk goes on. If, however, we could stop and take a moment, we might see what we have to do with the pain instead of being led by our minds telling us we haven't got time. Pain can be emotion that we haven't let go of; we hold onto it in the body and eventually it has to come out and it does in the way of pain. So rather than ask where the pain is coming from, maybe we should ask "What emotion am I holding onto I need to let go of? Of course we have to be willing to do this, and we need to be ready. Not everyone will want to or be ready, that is where I can help a lot of my clients. There are going to be times when the pain is due to a medical or surgical emergency, say and appendix or gall stones. In all instances the pain does need to be checked out medically. If nothing shows up in tests and no one is able to give you a reason as to where the pain is coming from, then you look at what emotion am I holding onto?

Quite often I will ask a client, "How does it make you feel? How do you feel?" The answer generally comes from their head as they are thinking about their answer, not feeling it. So they will say things like, "I think if feels alright." The key word here is "think," which shows me they are coming from the mind; they are thinking it rather than feeling it. As humans, everything has to be logical because that is how we think and function. It's almost like we have forgotten how to feel; we are too scared to really go there. Of course we function in our everyday lives; we have jobs, friends, marriages, children, and so on. We can all function, but deep down beneath those layers there is a volcano waiting to erupt and we just keep adding to it by not acknowledging our true feelings and forgetting about our heart and using our head. Our heart is the feeling centre; our mind is the thinking centre. We can't say how we are feeling from our head; it just doesn't work because it's way too logical. We say one thing yet our body is not able to feel it. If we are not able to feel it in our body we start to switch off, and our body becomes foreign to us. This is when we need to reconnect with our bodies and heart; we need to feel again, which means we need to start to clear away the entire emotional trauma we have hidden. Clearing emotion brings us back to having everything in balance. We need our minds, but we need them in the capacity they are designed for, to think. Minds are not designed to feel, that is the heart's job. To help us get to where we are today our minds have done the job of the heart, otherwise we would have folded generations ago. Now, however, we are getting a bit smarter (excuse the pun) and we are starting to realise just how important the heart actually is, and not just for pumping out the blood which keeps us alive. We need to bring the heart back into balance with the body and mind and for the three to work together again. The mind has been in control for too long and it's now time for the mind to hand some of that responsibility back to the heart. When this happens we will be living in our bodies, we will be feeling again and our mind will be thinking what it is designed for. It will no longer need to do the work of the mind and heart; it can solely concentrate on its own work. Some new age books talk about dismissing the mind, but this isn't possible: we need the mind just as much as we need the heart. It's about bringing back balance and being in equilibrium once again.

Remember when I gave the examples of Jay asking me how I felt, and how I wanted to move but couldn't, and how I almost blew a gasket when telling people what I thought of them on the course? I was able to do all of that safely as I came from the heart. Prior to that my words and actions would have been from the mind and would not have had such an impact on me as they did coming from the heart. The heart is our true centre, this is the hub of where all life comes from. Imagine living life coming from the heart, without being hurt or wounded as we have cleared away all negative emotion. Now we are starting to live and see how life should and can be if we allow ourselves not to be ruled by our minds. It is time to bring it all back into balance.

I would like to add another part to this, it's not just about the heart and mind it's also about the other organs we have in the body as well. They are just as vital in storing held on emotions, and so the heart is only one part of it. For instance, according to some philosophies like the Chinese, Kidneys hold onto fear, stomach holds onto anxiety, liver holds onto anger. If you look at the body that way it is so fascinating, the body has and is showing us the answers, but are we listening? It is always about keeping everything in balance and working back to restore balance. Every system in our body, every part of our body is there for a reason. The mind is a wonderful tool, but we are limiting our access to its full possibilities. We limit ourselves by being stuck in our emotions and letting them rule, once we come away from there, we can open up our minds even higher and start to see the full potential it holds, for us to use, if we want to.

# Chapter Eleven
## The ability of self-heal

*Follow what you believe to be true*
*Follow yourself.*

As mentioned in previous chapters our body holds onto everything that happens to us, not only in this lifetime but from previous lifetimes we have had as well (of course not everyone will believe in past lives, it doesn't matter). Quite often if there is something happening in our lives or body we can't make sense of, it doesn't fit with what we do and we don't know where it has come from, then guaranteed it has been carried over from a previous life. I believe even though we die and our physical body decomposes, our energy is still carried over into the next life we choose to have. As a youngster I was petrified of heights. I remember once we were in South Germany and we caught a cable car to the top of the Alps I was absolutely shaking going up on it and when we reached the top I had to sit down because my knees and body were shaking so much. When I was learning to ski I was again petrified of being up on the mountain. As strange as it might sound, I kept feeling I was going to fall off the mountain. Then, a long time later, as previously mentioned, I had a session with Soul Recovery where I was shown I had indeed been a female mountain climber back in 1900s and, at the age of twenty-six, I had fallen through a crevice to my death.

Now I understood the feeling I had experienced. I had actually died on a mountain, so it was no wonder that feeling of extreme fear still existed. I knew it didn't make sense for this lifetime, but until the session I didn't know where it came from. So I believe we do carry the energy of our soul over into each lifetime, we just have a different physical body. Please remember this is my take on it, and my theory is based on the personal experience I have had. There are of course other authors and philosophies out there who say similar things; it all comes down to personal belief.

Soul Recovery was really interesting. One session would last me for a year and I had four sessions in total. So over the four years I was having them I started to put the pieces of my soul back together, and have continued to do so since. The energy is carried over, this I have mentioned. But when something dramatic/ traumatic happens to us, our soul leaves our bodies; it's too hard to deal with, just like when we are not present in our bodies. If we don't get the soul piece back, then there is a part of us that is missing. Have you ever had the feeling you're just not quite right, something is missing, but you can't put your finger on it, well it could be because part of your soul is missing. Gradually we can reclaim the pieces; we have to reclaim them as part of our healing. We can't fully heal until all parts of us are brought back together. To heal we need to be present in our body, and to do this we need to be grounded and aware of our emotions, not running scared of them. We need to be present, for that is where the learning happens. Many authors have talked about being present to be able to heal. *"The Power of Now"*, by Eckhart Tolle talks exactly about being present, in the Now, to help you heal. How, we are so busy looking forward we actually miss the present, and it's in the Now we receive the help we need. When we ask questions we receive the answer in the Now, but we are too busy to hear or see what we are being told. I liked it as it put a simple explanation on things one for me made sense at the time. A lot of this work can be confusing at times. This book touched those spots that helped answer lots of questions I had in a simple way. Remember though, if you're not quite ready when you read the book, you won't like what the author has to say. Don't dismiss it as rubbish: keep it to read at a later date when you find yourself more ready to hear what is said. Everything is about timing, the time must be right! That goes for any book you read, never dismiss it, and just hold onto it until you are ready to get those answers from it.

Again not everyone will believe what I have just written, and that's absolutely fine. The ideas are hard to get your head around, and of course we all believe and think differently. But if there is a notion of knowing, "Hey that's makes sense," but you have no idea why, then that's what you go with, your gut instinct. When we follow our gut instinct we don't always have to understand why it is so. Remember, with some of this work there is no manual to say what is the right or wrong way. There are no rules, except you should come from a place of love and respect for yourself and your fellow man, and you do for the greater good of all not just to benefit yourself, that's all.

We are governed by rules in everyday life so when it comes to spiritual matters we expect the same. However, there aren't any, so we can find a spiritual path hard to follow to start off with, I know I certainly did. After being nursing for twenty-seven years where there is a manual that sets out the way to do everything, to doing my inner work where I needed to follow what felt right, or allowing me to be guided in what to do was certainly very foreign territory. To start with I would question all the time and wonder if I was doing things the right way. Each time I questioned I had a deep knowing I was doing the right thing, yet I didn't really understand how or why, how I knew this. It's not until we start to clear our own emotional blocks and trauma that we can start to see clearly and certainly understand that bit more. I will still question my path on a very rare occasion, but mostly I follow, trust and do, and know that's what it is. To many it will seem weird, bizarre and they might even think I need to be locked up in a strait jacket (as was one suggested by a friend!). To me, however, it's my normal reality, whatever normal is!

I am re reading a book by Bruce Lipton called *Spontaneous Evolution* which is really fascinating and certainly gets the old brain going if we are open to it. At the end of one of the chapters Lipton writes, "Believing is seeing," a twist on the old saying, "Seeing is Believing." Lipton's version absolutely struck home for me this time as I don't quite think I grasped it as I should have the first time I read it. This time I fully understood what he meant. Once we believe, then we see, we see all, we see what truly is there not we have been led to believe is there. Science has us thinking if we can't see something then it's not true. Even my partner agrees with this. He wants to be shown the truth, but the only truth lies in what we believe to be true for ourselves not what we have been programmed to be believe in, been duped or hypnotized to believe in. So each person's truth will be different from another person as we are all individuals. Trying to show the truth means we are all trying to fit into the same shape, like a square, but we are also circles, oblongs and triangles so we will never all fit into the same shape, and we will never all have the same truth. And remember that truth certainly can't be shown it needs to be felt. Asking for it to be shown means you are coming from the logical brain, the mind is trying to make sense of things so we can understand, but to understand something we need to feel it; believe it, and then we will see it.

It was strange for me to re- read this book as it jumped out at me in the library and initially I thought I had read it, but I was told, "No," so I borrowed it. When I got home and I realised I had actually read it, so why on earth was I reading it again, especially after I had been told by my guides I had to stop reading all books, newsletters, everything, so I did. It was a hard thing to do as I loved reading and books have always been my saving grace as it was through them I started to open up my eyes more, so you can see why this was a hard task for me. But stop I did, as by now I was catching on fast and it was time to start to listen what my own guides were telling me. I accepted that what I get told is what I do, no questions asked. So imagine my surprise when I was in the library and I had the urge to read this particular book. I kept reminding myself I wasn't meant to be reading, but I was drawn to the book, so I borrowed it. There were two reasons for me to borrow this book, the first being I related this book to two clients I recently had seen. The second was I was being reminded there is still information in it I missed the first time, I am hopefully getting this time round. So even though I knew not to read, I followed my instinct and borrowed this book I was being led to again and went with it. It seems the reading wasn't just going to benefit me this time. So there are no rules, you go by what feels right and what you are guided to do.

Now of course this doesn't leave it open for people to go out and harm people, or steal or do anything like that just because it feels "right" to do, please be sure I am *not* saying that. As mentioned before, if we come from love, respect and love of self and fellow man, then we are okay. Being harmful, vindictive and stealing are actions that come from the ego. They are actions to make the person feel better about themselves in terms of their ego and a sense of me; it's all about me, me, me. Such actions do not allow a person to empower themselves in a healthy way. There are certainly people out there who work under the umbrella of helping people, but all they are doing is feeding their own ego, making you feel they are the only person who can help you. They are not operating from a position of love. Rather, they are motivated by ego. Helping people is about assisting them to empower themselves with their own healing energies and wonderful gifts that we each have but have not yet accessed. Helping others is about guiding and encouraging them to follow their own instinct rather than using the approach of "What I say is gospel." This approach when working with others ends up with that person relying on you to tell them what to do, and when we do this we hand over our power to others. Doing this work is about showing and allowing others to heal themselves, teaching they are capable of doing it themselves by following their own guides, and encouraging them to trust themselves to do what feels right for them and not blindly doing what others tell them to do. We can best help others to do their own healing by enriching them as they do it.

Each of us has the ability to heal ourselves, it's just we have never been told we can, and if we had we wouldn't really believe it as we are so reliant on others to help us and seem to have lost the ability to help ourselves. We each know our own body better than anyone in any medical or new age field, as it is our body. We have been programmed to be numb to our body and our feelings and so we have lost touch with the ability to heal ourselves. We can reclaim this back if we want to. We expect others to make us happy or to make us better. Wrong! Other people may guide or assist us but the end results need to come from us. We need to do the hard yards, we need to wake up and realise the only person who can help us is us, no one else. We need to stop handing over our power to others thinking they know best for us, when they don't. We are all individuals and while we may come from the same place, we each have our own body and bodies come in different shapes, sizes. We have our own unique fingerprints do we not, which shows we are individuals. Yet we like to think we are all the same, that one size fits all, but it doesn't. One therapy may work for one person but it doesn't mean it will work for the next person. We need to find what works for us and follow it. When we go the doctor, if any of the symptoms we describe don't fit in their tick box then they don't know how to help us and are quick to say nothing can be done. If you are lucky your doctor may refer you onto another specialist, or recommend an alternative kind of treatment, which is great, but there are no guarantees it will work for you. You need to gauge what you and your body like and don't like and notice how it reacts to different treatments. The one that works best for you and your body is what you go with, that is what you follow. Of course you need to be open to this idea, and certainly there are lots of different therapies and modalities out there that can you can google and try.

It's almost like we have forgotten how to think for ourselves when it comes to our own body and being. We have been given so many different rules and regulations, is it any wonder we can't think for ourselves. But what if there weren't any rules. Would we still survive and what would we do? Of course we would survive, it's just the authorities would like you to think that you couldn't and there would be mayhem and disorder. Not that long ago I watched a nature program that showed how a colony of animals survived. The ant was the smallest in size but had the largest number in the colony. The colony was very organized and there was no leader, yet everything had a flow and there was no disruption. There was no top dog dishing out orders. Of course people would say that's ants, we're humans, but maybe we should look and follow how other species survive with no rules, regulations or top dog. It's definitely worth thinking about if, of course, we can get our heads around the idea of alternative ways of doing things; after all we have been programmed for so long. There is so much we are not aware of as of our minds/head haven't allowed us to be open to the alternatives. This can change once we come from our heart again and start feeling things out rather than thinking things out! Imagine the spin our poor heads would be in then! But for the better of all

# Chapter Twelve
## Honour our ancestors

*To all our ancestors who were pioneers of their time, protectors of the land and their own Healers, I thank you.*

Last year I was taking our dog for a walk at our usual spot by the river. I quite often get a feeling I need to go there. As we walked I just started shouting. Noises I have never heard before were coming out of my throat. As the energies got stronger the sound coming out wasn't my voice. It felt like it went deeper than that, somehow it felt like it was the voice of my ancestors. It felt like I had connected with my ancestors. I walked away thinking, "That was strange!" but felt good. I say I connected with my ancestors because as the sound echoed it went deeper than anything I have ever felt, or known. It was a sound I have never heard of before and it took me to the inner core of my soul. That's about the only way I can try to describe it. It was very cathartic indeed. So I found myself repeating this experience on the odd occasion when I needed to. Each time was always different, but I was always in the same spot by the river.

Then later on in the year I did a workshop on finding your voice and it felt like all the work I had been doing previously by the river was preparing me for this workshop. The workshop was very powerful and afterwards I started using my bongos and sound a lot more. I was beginning to connect with sound; I even started using sound in my healing sessions as that was what I was being guided to do. I was definitely reconnecting with someone or something; I just wasn't too sure what.

Last night I had a healing session, and today as I sit here and write, I discovered I had been protecting my heart from getting hurt for so long, many lifetimes actually. I knew I had done this, but not to the extent it was revealed to me. I always thought I had a brick wall around my heart, but no, I actually had steel bars. At least that explained why the bricks weren't coming down, even after all the work I have done on this lifetime's inner child. But then I was told it's the core of my inner child that is behind the bars and suddenly the penny dropped. I had been doing work on the inner child from this lifetime, I had forgotten I had more than one inner child. Of course I did, all those other lifetimes of abuse and everything else that went with them. Now I understood and now I knew what to work with. To help me move forward I had to bring my core inner child away from the bars. She was hiding and using the bars for protection, she was that scared. With the work that had been done the previous night, and the work I was doing the day after, I saw the bars dissolve, just disappear and an amazing white light came in and out and filled up the whole of me, it was amazing. I knew my core inner child was with me. To finalize the process I had to go for a walk and ended up at my usual spot by the river. While walking I was singing and this time the noises coming out of my throat were different again but it felt okay. The sound was still coming from my ancestors, my core, and my soul. It felt like I had reconnected with my soul.

Afterwards I remembered about how it all began with me going to the river and singing, then the course and now this and I realised everything was connected and it had to be done that way. Everything I had done so far had been leading me up to this day. So even though at the time I didn't know why I had to do it, I just knew I was meant to, and so I did. Now the final piece of the puzzle fitted into place. Everything happens for a reason, at the right time and at the right place, when you are ready. This example I hope has just shown how that works. Follow your instinct and you will never go wrong, never. After all gut instinct is spirit's way of guiding us. I never realised that until a friend told me a few weeks ago, of course, why wouldn't it be.

Now I could explain a bit more about gut instinct and why it was so important to follow. For those who may read this and say, "Yes it worked out for you, but how do I know if it would work for me?" my answer to that is you wouldn't be told to do something if it wasn't going to work out for you, but it also has to do with what your expectations are. Just remember to keep an open mind and don't have any expectations for they will cause you to fall, which defeats the object of following your instinct. If you have no expectations then you accept more of what has happened than if you had an idea of how it should have been. Let that idea of expectation go for it is that thought that is stopping you. Trust and follow and you will always be guided and be shown what way to go next.

Home! Where is home? For some it's the place where they grew up and have raised their own children, that's their home, their sense of belonging. I have always struggled with that question, with dad in the Army we moved around a lot so I never had an answer. Then

146

when I moved to New Zealand I claimed Edinburgh as home for I felt connected to that place, had spent time there as a child and later on had done some of my nurse training there, so Edinburgh it was. But I still struggled with that question, even though I finally had an answer, I knew it wasn't quite right, I knew there was more to it, just didn't know what. Most of my life I have travelled from city to city, country to country looking, searching, not finding and moving on, that's how it was. The song by Paul Young, "Wherever I lay my hat, that's my home" always rang true for me whenever I thought about where is home. Then, when I stepped on the shores of New Zealand, I felt something different. I felt a familiarity and I have no idea how as I had only been here once on holiday for a week prior to that. Yet the feeling was there.

When I moved to Dunedin, the Edinburgh of the south, it was hard not to think of it as home, after all it was Edinburgh, but in a different way. So I stayed there for five years, successfully breaking many life cycles in the meantime. Then I moved to Alexandra in Central Otago and things really did start to move and change for me there. I remember when I first drove into Alexandra I was escorted by three hawks and the words "Welcome home" rang clearly. Of course I took that meaning literally and thought at last I had a place to call home. Imagine to my confusion when eighteen months later I packed up and left. "How could I have gotten it so wrong?" I wondered. Wrong to the point that before I left Dunedin I had bought all new furniture in order to set myself up in my little unit in Alexandra because I felt so sure I was finally going to settle. Eighteen months later, however, I sold it all and lost a lot of money as a result. I promised myself I would never do that again, and I haven't. There was a big lesson for me to learn from that experience. A few months prior to leaving Alexandra, I realised I was living my life as a married person, but without a husband or children. What was I doing? I was single and should be out exploring. I also realised during this time I was working to pay for my rent and didn't have much left afterwards. It was time for a change. I resigned from my job, and let my landlord know I would be leaving. I was going to travel NZ in a camper van and all the small places I never had the time to stop at. I planned to pick up casual work as a nurse or massage therapist. I was excited by the idea of travelling again.

So I was all packed and ready to go, when I met Lyndsay. I moved in with him after knowing him for a month. I did end up travelling, but it was across the ditch to Australia, not around New Zealand as I had planned. Everyone thought I was mad; expect my mum, who was more than pleased I had finally met a man and, I guess in her eyes at least, was deemed to be normal now! She was also very happy I wouldn't be travelling around by myself as she didn't like the thought of it.

I discovered while in Australia I really missed New Zealand, especially Central Otago; for me there is something very special about that place. So when Aimee was about nine months old we moved back to Central and have been here ever since. New Zealand is home, no doubt about it, but Scotland is also home, after all that is where my ancestors are, that is my birthplace. I felt a similar connection when I was on holiday in Canada, it felt like New Zealand just in a bigger scale. There are many places I haven't visited and I have no doubt when I do some of them will feel like home too. So I guess what I am trying to say is no one place has to be home, there can be a few, as I am discovering. I guess the next question then is, "How can that be?" I'm no expert, but to my way of thinking, in many places the land is very old, while some countries are newer than others, like New Zealand it is relatively younger in history compared to Britain. The energies of the land and the ancestors of the land are still held within the land and we are connected to it all. We are all connected to every bit of nature, every animal and everything on the planet. A lot of authors of new age books talk about this. I feel however, it is hard to get your head around a concept like this. The more I discover about myself and move away from my limiting beliefs, the more I change within myself and with this change I find myself beginning to understand. Each time I ask a question I am expecting a clear, logical answer from the mind. This isn't possible, for there is no clear logical answer; it is what we feel it is. So when I was told "welcome home" when I was escorted in by three hawks into Alexandra I took that literally, meaning to stay. Eighteen months later I moved away thinking I had got it wrong. I hadn't, that was the start of my journey coming home. Coming home to the real me, remembering what everything is about. Discovering more and more about the process of life, and finding out about the mysteries of what we call life. Each time I discover new things about myself I open up more to a new possibility of life. I open up to a new way of thinking and being. So you see, home is where the heart is, for wherever you are that is home. It isn't about being in one physical place all the time, as what I thought, it is wherever you are and go. There is no right or wrong, or logical answer it is just what it is.

During the workshop of finding your voice, which was based on Native American beliefs, I was given a green quartz bear which was hugely significant for me. While travelling through Canada many years beforehand I was sat outside a book shop when a big bear face appeared in front of me. I kept shaking my head as I thought I was seeing things. But each time I opened my eyes it would still be there. It turned out to be one of my spirit guide animals and her name was Orla; this was the first time I had actually seen anything so real, yet untouchable if you see what I mean! That was the start of my many spirit animals coming in to let me know they were there walking beside me.

I had many different experiences when I was on different lands in Canada. When I was on a bus traveling through the Rockies I looked up at a big mountain and on the face of the peak were the faces of four Indian chiefs. I saw them as clear as day; I still see that image today. Sometimes when I look at pictures the whole picture can change, into something quite different. Once I said this to a friend in New Zealand and she seriously said I should go to the doctor and get checked out, as it wasn't normal. Of course it's not normal to how we are trained to perceive it, but what if that was more normal than what we thought? One day, while still in Canada, I visited an old French settlement and walked into what would have been the Church. It felt really cold and horrible and I had to get out of there fast. Then I walked into another building which felt lovely and warm and inviting. There was a lady in this building who was telling stories to some children who had come to visit. While standing there I could see a fire burning. There were lots of different beds around the whole of the room and the colours of a bright yellow and orange played on the walls. The room had an amazing feeling and I instantly felt safe. After a few minutes I looked up and was back in the building of "today." There was no fire, no beds and no colours. I then realised I had been shown what the room had been used for in the past. The local Indians used to sleep there with their furs wrapped around them; it felt amazing. This was all new to me, and for a while I thought I was imagining things. Eventually, however, I began to accept it must be real. Years before when I was in Scotland I stood on the old battlefield of Culloden and could hear all the screaming and fighting. The energy of the place wasn't good at all, which is not surprising considering it was one of the many big battlefields from history. I had to walk away quickly as I felt quite strange and eerie. Here in Canada similar things were happening, so I had to start to believe they were real and true.

I had the chance to revisit the battlefield of Culloden a couple of months ago. I went with a purpose and a knowing. Walking around this time felt totally different to my last visit. There were no battle cries, or eerie feeling it felt a lot calmer and I knew healing had occurred on the land. I felt privileged to be walking on those lands knowing what had occurred centuries ago.

The experiences I was having seemed to happen wherever I went, it was now I was beginning to realize what was happening. I was becoming aware and no longer shrugging them off as my imagination. While visiting the west coast of New Zealand I visited one of the lakes and as I walking around I suddenly saw two Native American Indians running around, one was a girl and the other a man. The girl I had been before and there was lots of laughter and play. I was told then my name was Runs With Wind. At first I thought that's not a name, but the words were very clear and not knowing what I was to do with any of this information, I just accepted it. I now had an interest in Native American Indian beliefs and spiritual beliefs and was keen to learn. I loved their philosophy of life and how they incorporated nature into everything. They honoured all aspects of being, particularly their ancestors, and they have a lot of respect for their elders. For a while I was right into learning and practicing what they did. But then I moved on and discovered the ways of other cultures and researching other philosophies, but I never forgot how I started off with the American Indians. So when I attended the workshop to find my voice, I didn't really know what to expect. I was blown away when I was given the bear. I felt like I was being given permission to carry on the work I am doing. The gift of the bear was also like being told this is real, all the experiences you have had are real; I am proof. I felt as though I had done a full circle as part of my journey had started off with the image of the bear in Canada and now I had completed the circle and the bear was being given to me as a gift to use. Whatever I was meant to do, now was the time to start and to continue the work and believe in what I am doing, for it is more real than what we call reality today that we live in. I am still working with now, she is grandmother bear, she is a healer and teacher, and she is the mother of all mothers. She has the knowledge and wisdom of those all gone by, she will help me to open up my heart and be centred in my own body.

Over summer we quite often pack up and go camping. It's a great way to relax, chill and not do much except admire the scenery we are fortunate to be surrounded by. On one of these occasions we went to some lakes that are extremely spiritual. While registering at the campground I took a moment to admire the magnificent start of the lake. I was aware of a presence and was thankful to be there. I then saw a huge face appear over the lake and was told she was the grandmother of the lake. By now I was accustomed to these types of things happening and wondered what else was going to happen while I was there. Quite a lot as it turned out, but in a very subtle way of course. I got really mad on one occasion, which is something I don't like doing. I worked with the anger by doing some writing where things started to be made clearer to me.

I was connecting with the land, and I could feel the energy of the land. At that point the land wasn't very happy as it felt that people take advantage of it and we're taking it for granted. They use and abuse it, they don't ask for permission or check to see if it's okay to walk up it hills or mountains. People think it is their right to talk and make lots of noise rather than being quiet and listening to the land for a change. What also came up was the dumping of rubbish. As I am sitting writing this now initially I thought the concerns the land has was to do with physical rubbish, but I actually think it is a lot more than that. I think it has to do with dumping of psychological rubbish on the land. When I say this I mean what people are thinking, their thoughts, all of this goes into the land depending on what type of mood they are in, and the land holds onto all of this. Now of course this happens without us being aware of it, but it goes in hand in hand with what I have been saying so far: we need to be aware of our thoughts, beliefs and how they affect not only us and those around us, but the land we are standing on as well. Funnily enough I was told to write about rubbish and how the land feels. An interesting ask I thought but I tried, and each time I tried I didn't getting very far as I couldn't connect with rubbish. Again I had taken it literally by thinking physical rubbish. When, after all that time, I considered psychological rubbish I finally understood what was meant. This is yet again another example of even when we don't understand what we are told to do, it will make sense in the end. When we are told to do something there is a reason and a purpose, but we are generally blocked to seeing that by our expectations. My expectation in this case was thinking only of physical rubbish, but it wasn't so until I had cleared that block I could fully understand what I was mean to do.

After that trip I never touched alcohol again. Up to then I had been only having the odd glass of wine compared to what I used to drink, but I was still having a glass. I had made a conscious decision while on that trip not to drink anymore, as I was aware I no longer liked the way it made me feel. I also felt that as I was working closer with Spirit, I really shouldn't let anything interfere with that, so alcohol had to go. At the time I didn't think much about my decision. A few months later I started to join the dots together and realised a lot more had gone on when I was at the lake than I had first realised. With her energy, the grandmother of the lake, of the land, had helped me realise I no longer needed to drink. Four years on and I still haven't touched a drop of alcohol, and the best thing is I don't want to, don't need to and certainly don't miss it. I can now function alcohol free and still have a good time. In fact I feel heaps better. So as you see, it can be done, it is all about timing, trusting and following.

I believe we cannot heal ourselves until we heal the land. The land is so ancient it holds onto everything single thing that happens, so everything that has occurred over time, the land is still holding onto now. With each generation I think we are beginning to lose the connection we once had with the land. Our ancestors had that close connection and that is why I think more of them are now coming to the forefront to help us. If we connect with our ancestors and connect with the land it will benefit not only us as individuals but the whole of mankind. What I am beginning to discover is that a lot of the ancestors want to make right, things that transpired when they were around, but which were never attended to in their lifetimes. A lot are realizing they need to correct, make amends for things that went wrong in their time and now is the time to heal it all. As mentioned heal the land, and then we can heal ourselves. So even though New Zealand is a relatively new land compared to Britain, it still holds onto all things that happened to it before the arrival of man and since man came to inhabited it. We need to realise what we do to the land is important.

It continues to amaze me that here I am, a white female of foreign descent dealing with spiritual matters in an amazing country that has its own spiritual culture. Yet it is a country and a culture I feel really connected with. Then again I feel connected with the Native American culture and I feel connected with the Indian culture. I feel connected with the Druids, my original roots where I come from, and the list goes on and will continue to go on as I maintain to learn and grow from all knowledge I gain!

## Chapter Thirteen
## Words do matter

*Words can be wonderful or cutting, they can pick you up*
*or drop you like a hot brick*
*Either way words do matter*

When I was younger I would never say a bad word about anyone. I always gave them the benefit of the doubt or made excuses for them. I would never look for the worst in people. I even made excuses for my dad and was always saying things like, "It's not his fault," or "He gets nagged at." I guess I saw mum as the one to blame for his behaviour. Maybe if she talked to us a bit more when we were kids I wouldn't have thought that, but as a child you don't know any different. It was only as I got older and I guess the reality of things started to creep in, innocence of child leaving, cynicism of adult starting to seep in. With that brought negative thoughts to the forefront and they started to take over, I don't actually remember when but know they did. Gone was the belief I saw good in everything and everyone. What started to take over was seeing the negative in everything and everyone. The rot set in, the damage was done and it stayed that way for a long time. It's like a slow decline in the person you could have been, the person you should be, and if we never wake up we never see it happening or are aware it is there.

The easiest way of going into a slow decline is by gossiping, and boy do we all love to gossip. We love to talk about another person, what they did or didn't do how they behave, what they wore and what they said. The old programmes like *The Midwife*, which are set in post war England, show everyone in a close proximity of each other, everyone knowing each other business and everyone gossiping about each other. When we ask why they do this there are numerous reasons including simply passing the time of day, making you feel better about yourself if you can see someone who is worse off than your or for a moment it takes you away from your own unhappy life. We give ourselves permission to gossip by justifying it with comments like, "it's just women helping each other," or "what we like to do is talk." So gossiping has been deemed as being a normal part of life. But is it? Should it be and is it really alright to talk about others?

What we say about ourselves to ourselves, and what we say about others is very significant and it matters a lot more than what we realise. The small chatter that goes on in our heads is damaging to our whole physical being, for our subconscious believes what we tell it. Our subconscious has no sense of humour; it literally believes everything we tell it. So when we say, "I'm no good at that," or "I'm useless, no one loves me," the subconscious literally believes those words and it thinks we are telling it the truth. This is how damaging words are to us and therefore the rest of society in general. So when we gossip about others we are being negative and, as a result, we are constantly subjecting our subconscious to negativity. It can't tell if we are joking or not, or if we didn't really mean it, what we tell our subconscious is what it will take literally. So words are important, they are crucial to how we can function effectively as a human being. Once again, when we talk in a negative way we are coming from fear, from the ego. When we talk and act positively we are coming from love, from our heart. Of course some people will act as if they are happy and smile a lot, but deep down they're not, it's just they are fooling themselves no one else. It is not enough to speak and act in a positive way, you must believe it, you must feel it, and hence you will be it. Words are not enough just by themselves to change things, but words are critical to our being on the whole. Negative words are the beginning of the rot that can set into our souls; they have the power to blow out the light that we may have had flickering inside of us. When we stop talking about others, ourselves, in a negative manner, then how your view of yourself and the world can change.

As you have read in earlier chapters one of my demons was hearing and thinking people are talking about me. However, did my experience stop me from talking about others? No of course not; I still joined in and was as guilty as everyone else. Sometimes when I did gossip it felt like a relief off my shoulders, especially if someone had been bugging me, as it was good to learn others may have felt the same way. So I felt better afterwards, did it make it right? At the time I would have thought so, but now I know it wasn't right.

We need to start to be more tolerant and accepting of others. As a society in general I don't think we do that very well. Even when you look back at history we have never done it very well, so we haven't really learnt very much or moved on have we, not in the social sense anyway. We need to come from love and not fear. When we gossip we come from fear characterized by a lower vibration of energy. When we come from love we are in the higher vibration energy and that is what we need to aim and strive for if we are going to change.

This of course is a lot easier said than done and I struggle personally with that, but I am working on it. I don't do well in groups; sometimes people scare me, just like life can scare me. I guess it's no wonder with everything that happened to me, but I know I can, and must change the way I relate to others if I am to grow and move forward. It's not been easy doing that and sometimes I am successful in ignoring what my own inner voices are telling me and resort to the paranoia, "she must be talking about me," or "she is saying this about me." Remember this is how I have only ever known it, until now. What I am now learning and working with is when this happens I breathe myself through saying, "its okay, everything's alright." One example of how I am learning to change is when we were away camping with friends I had come back from a walk and my friend was talking with another person she had met. They both looked over at me and said something I couldn't hear. Well that set off my alarm bells; every single bell you could think of was ringing in my head. "Here we go again," I thought. I instantly went into panic/fear mode which could see me being short, not really talking to anyone else and certainly not saying what had just happened and how I had taken it. Based on past experience I had the potential to stay in this mode for days. However, this time I went and lay down by the lake and managed to change the thought around in my head to, "This is okay. I can thank them because if it wasn't for them I wouldn't be going through this and all it is doing is showing me I still have some stuff to clear but I'm still not quite there." I kept saying this over and over until I could finally feel a change starting to happen, I had managed to change the energy of the thought around and it wasn't affecting me as it would have in the past. So rather than holding onto for days or weeks, I was able to let it go literally within half an hour. From there I was able to carry on and function as I would normally have. I know this doesn't sound a lot, but for me it is. So you see, no matter what your issue is it might not seem much to others but to the person going through it is it huge. Remember, it can be changed and all you need to do is change the thought around it, but you need to be aware of it in the first place to change it.

With wanting and trying to fit in socially, I tend to find I also try and pre-empt what might happen next, or be one step ahead of a person by trying to anticipate what they will say or do so nothing comes as a surprise to me. I have always felt the need to have some control over. Doing this means I can never relax when I am in company of other people as I am too busy looking around, seeing, watching, guessing and pre-empting. I'm not sure what happened to just enjoying the moment where you are at, listening and talking to others without always being on the lookout.

Some may see this type of behaviour as not being friendly or sociable, which is probably right, but not for the reasons they might think. As far back as I can remember I have always done this, thinking it's normal and believing others do the same. However, once I realised others don't do this I tried to figure out why I done that. I had a session with Jay and I was telling her about it. She was able to shed some light by saying the behaviour I was displaying all came down to being abused. When you have been abused you are always on the lookout for what will happen next so you can feel you have some control over it. Being a victim of abuse you have no control over anything, you are powerless. So by acting this way you can feel you are taking control and are at times in control, except, of course, it is very damaging. If things don't go right you also blame yourself; which is another example of what you think about yourself if you have been abused. When she told me all this it made sense, but I was left wondering how to change this behaviour, as I have never felt comfortable in social situations with people around me. I'm okay one to one but not with a group of people. In the past I would have said I 'm just not comfortable with them. Now I know I can feel and sense everyone's energy, which is too overloading for me and can send me into a spin.

Remember change doesn't occur overnight, it takes a lot of work on mainly your inner self as you get in touch with your demons, shed the light on them and let them go. It is a slow process but one that works. Now I can be with a crowd of people, as I have got stronger within myself and understand a bit more I don't let it get to me as much as it would have in the past. Sometimes it can be plain sailing while other times can be very choppy, but generally on the choppy days it shows me there is still something which I need to go into in order to release it. Now I don't blame myself if I say something wrong, or think others don't like me. I try not to go there but if I do, then I wipe it out of my head by saying, "It's okay, they might have lots happening for them," or I go into my inner self to see what is coming up for me as generally that is the way it shows me I have another demon raising its head and needs to be let go of.

Remember back in Chapter One I wrote about not being able to do small talk very well. This doesn't help me much either in social situations, especially when some people can start talking about everything and anything. Such people tend to dominate a conversation and be the life and soul of the party. Yet, if you stop and look at them, they have just as many issues as everyone else does just different ones. While it takes a whole combination of people to make the world go round, you need to be comfortable with who you are and what makes you tick. When you accept your good points and not so good points, and accept everyone else's as well, life will be a lot easier and simpler. My point being we can't have a room full of people who dominate a conversation, we need a combination of people; we also need listeners. I am a listener and I'm okay with that now!

One of the biggest revelations is that throughout my whole life I have been trying to fit in by drinking, socializing, gossiping etc. But really it's been like trying to fit a square peg into a round hole, it won't go no matter how hard you force and try, it won't fit. Trying to fit in, be accepted and be classed as normal is hard work. Whatever happened to being happy with whom you are? It is ironic there is so much pressure to fit in when most people really want to be just accepted for who they are. Only now am I starting to feel comfortable in my own skin. I finally feel as though I don't have to try anymore. This is who I am, this is who I am becoming and if people don't like that they won't stay, and I am truly fine with that. It's taken a long time but it I feel like I am getting there, and others can as well, if they want to.

## Chapter Fourteen
## Damage to our psyche

*Love makes the world go round.*

A lot of my worry and expectation around people talking about me is to do with disbelief in myself. I have convinced myself over the years I am unlovable or even likeable, which is quite big when you think what we are meant to be about is all about love. So if, as I believed, others don't like me and I don't like myself, where does that leave space for love? All the space is taken up with loathing of self and with negative lower vibration energy instead of a higher vibration of love; not just any love, but unconditional love.

To understand this we need to look at the law of attraction. If you keep saying and believing you are unlovable or unlikeable then you will attract people who don't love you, or for that matter even like you. In other words, what you think is what you will attract to you. Of course we may say things like, "Why does this always happen to me?" or, "I have had a bad run of blokes," or, "They don't treat me very well." Take note of what you have been saying to yourself and of what you expect to happen as a result of those thoughts. Do you really think there will be a happy ending if you keep saying negative things? Are you expecting things to fall apart like they have always done? Are you waiting to be hurt yet again?

This type of talk usually goes on in the subconscious so often you won't even be aware you think like this. So, before you can change things in your life, you have to become aware to what you think and say to yourself. After all, you can't change something if you are not conscious of it in the first place. The law of attraction holds true for absolutely everything we do in life: what we think is what we get. You have heard of the saying, "You are what you eat," well what if it became, "You are what you think." How can that phrase change the way you think about yourself? Just sit with these words for a minute and see what comes up for you!

When I was growing up I had a bottom drawer full of items I intended to use after I was married! There was an electric knife, tea towels and other things like that in it. As I reached the tender age of eighteen I suddenly wondered what on earth I was doing by saving all these things and realised I should be using them. So I took everything out of the drawer and the items were either used or given away. Once I had done I experienced a sense of freedom. I know that may sound strange but I guess part of me must have thought the normal thing to do in life was to get married and hence I had all the items needed for married life tucked away in my drawer. That sense of freedom I felt was because deep down I knew married life wasn't what I wanted.

What are we really taught when we are growing up? To answer this all you have to do is look at what books have been written and continue to be written for children today. Typically for girls the storyline is a man/prince will come along on his white charging horse to save the day and the maiden at the same time. So young girls get caught up in thinking a man will come along and save them, but in real life it really means marry them. By accepting the stories I was told when I was younger, I was waiting for a man to come and save me and so I had my drawer full for when I was married! Yet when I was six or seven I remember saying I wasn't going to get married until I had travelled the world. So why on earth did I have a drawer full of stuff in preparation for married life? I didn't want that as a child, yet here I was as a young adult believing this was what I wanted. Really I was showing signs of being caught up in what is deemed to be "normal" compared to what I really wanted. To be accepted as "normal" I expected a man to come along and "save" me. I kept telling myself that, "I'll be okay once I have met someone." I fully believed this must be true as that is what is written in all of the books is it not? Even today as I watch and listen to my daughter the same kind of thinking still exists. She recently said she wants to be a farmer when she grows up (along with a whole other list of other things as well). I told her she would have to marry a farmer as she knows nothing about farming. She immediately turned back to me and said, "No, I'll have my own farm and I'll get my friends to help me!" There was a little glimmer of hope she could be her own person without the notion of having to be saved.

My favourite movie as a child was *Wizard of Oz*. I loved that movie and would be glued to the TV watching it. I also loved the song "Somewhere Over the Rainbow" and in fact that is still one of my favourite songs today. As a child I thought that, as the movie had showed me, life would be better somewhere else, and I definitely hoped it was. While there was no prince in the movie, Dorothy and her friends thought the Wizard of Oz would fix all their problems and they had so much faith in this belief. However, they soon realised they could fix things for themselves and they didn't need anyone else to do it for them. To solve her own problems Dorothy had to believe in herself and soon realised home was actually where she wanted to be as she missed everyone. To get home she had to follow the Yellow Brick Road, which turned out to be the path she was meant to be on. As she travelled this road she found the answers she needed and met the people/guides who helped her on her way. Even now as I sit here writing this it has suddenly dawned on me that the movie has in fact a much deeper message for me beyond childhood enjoyment … I now realise it was telling me we need to follow our own instinct and believe in ourselves. I have just got that meaning now as I have written it down. Whatever Dorothy believed in could actually happen. I guess that is what I have been saying throughout this book it is up to us, no one else, just us.

Many times I have heard comments like, "once I get married I can change him," or "when I am married and I have someone to love me, life will be better." Yet how many times do marriages fail? Quite a lot it seems. I often wonder if we are getting married for the right reasons or are we doing it because that is what we have been told all these centuries to do. In other words do we really believe in it? At the time of course we do and I am sure some people will be shouting at this section of the book saying, "How absurd, of course marriage is right." If you are having a strong reaction to these words then that is what you really need to look at deep down when you are ready, not in the heat of the emotions, like now. Remember I'm not putting marriage down I'm just trying to show how duped women have been into thinking a man and marriage is the only way to be "saved," going by the stories we were told as children. Everyone loves the big wedding day, the dress, looking and feeling beautiful, and it's no wonder as that is all you see and hear in all the stories. Yet some can't handle the reality of what marriage is all about once the honeymoon is over. Many struggle with compromise, being open and realistic as it's not all about just us now. And of course he might not be the Mr Perfect we thought he was. Least of all, the problems we had are still there they haven't gone away, so now what do we do? The fairy-tale is over and reality starts to kick in. A number of marriages do last the distance, but many don't. For some it's no wonder as they have been expecting Prince Charming to make them feel better. The only person who can make us feel better is us, no one else, us and us alone. People don't want to hear that as it makes them feel scared for then they have no one else to blame but themselves. It's easy to be a victim and blame another person for then we don't have to take responsibility for ourselves.

Of course it's only now I realise we must save ourselves. Back when I was seventeen or eighteen I still thought I'd meet Mr Right and everything would be fine, but I wanted to have some fun first. I thought that a good time to settle down and have children would be around the age of twenty four or twenty five. Only problem was when that time came around I realised I wasn't ready to settle down as I was socializing and having a good time. So I convinced myself that twenty-nine or thirty would be a better age to have children as by then I would be ready to settle down. However, when I reached that age I was anything but ready for children. I was extremely depressed on my thirtieth birthday thinking I was really old because I was no longer in my twenties. No one was on the scene or even the horizon. I had a string of "he must be the one" relationships before each ended and I moved onto the next "he must be the one," and so it went on. By now I was wondering what was wrong with me because I didn't seem to be able to meet "Mr Right" while everyone around me was settling down. I fell further into depression I guess. Remember I had done counselling at age twenty-five and things had got better for a while, but not on the male side of things. The problem I had was I still held a light for an old flame. I knew we would have a few years apart as he was a few years younger than me but then I thought we would get back together; I just had that feeling. So every time I met someone they never matched up to him, so of course the relationship always failed. By the age of thirty I thought it was all over, into my thirties now no hope. This thinking still continued even after I went to New Zealand when I was thirty-two. There I had a string of unsuccessful relationships so a year later I decided, "That's it, no more males." So I swore off them as such. As it turns out, it was the best thing I have ever done. At the time I was looking after someone's place while she was overseas and had the place to myself, no distractions. All I had was time and space. Time and space to bring up my own inner demons, and that is what happened. Looking back now I realise if I had been with someone or had been flatting I wouldn't have allowed myself to do that. It didn't matter if I was feeling lousy or wanted to scream, or didn't want to talk I could. There was no one except me. Of course at the beginning I was still drinking but the more I got into my own stuff the less I needed to drink as things were clearing and I was starting to feel better.

I wasn't in too much of a rush to find the next guy to go out with as I was now quite attached to it just being me; I actually quite liked it. Of course I had friends who couldn't see it that way and wherever possible they would try and pair me up with a friend who just happened to be single and available! No, not interested was always my reply until I was out at lunch with work colleagues one Christmas and in walked a male and female. My friend went over and spoke with them and I remember wondering who the man was as my friend hadn't introduced me to him. Two days later I met that person and we have been together ever since. I moved to Australia to live with him after only knowing him for a month. This was a huge step in my life as I had never before lived with a male in a relationship. I was thirty-nine.

If I had not first let go my old flame, I am sure this relationship would never had happened as I wouldn't have been ready for it. I would not have accepted him for who he is, as my thinking would have been clouded by some idea or fantasy I had in my head as to who he should be and what I thought I wanted. After letting that notion go I was able to accept him for who he is, his own individual self.

When I met Lyndsay I had been doing a lot of inner work to find out who I was. If I hadn't done any of that, again I doubt I would have ended up with anyone as I had unrealistic expectations that the other person would love me then I would feel better about myself. Through my work I have learnt it doesn't work like that as you must learn to love yourself first. You can get into relationship thinking and expecting things in your life to get better, but what happens if your partner doesn't meet your expectations or worse you don't feel any better about life. There are times in fact when you can feel worse. What do you do then? Many people start arguing and blaming the other person. Really though, the unhappiness comes from you but often you are too entrenched to realise or own it for yourself.

Love and life are everything but at the beginning I didn't trust in life. I was scared of it, scared everything would come crashing down and my bubble would burst. I kept expecting everything that was good in my life would be taken away. That's what I believed. It took me a long time to realise life isn't really like this and it certainly doesn't have to be. Now I am more aware of what makes me tick, I take responsibility for what I think and say. There is a bigger picture we need to be aware of and we must understand everything happens for a reason. Now I believe this, life and love are a lot easier. Without a doubt there are still bumps on the road, but these bumps don't take me down anymore. Rather, I am just aware they are there. I need to continue to look at life and love to see what I need to let go of, what fears I am still holding onto and what I can let go of. To let the old go is to let in the new.

A different way of trying to explain how we come from fear and not love is the diagram below. This came to me when I was doing a session for a very good friend of mine, who also happens to be my sister from many lifetimes, and we have reconnected in this lifetime. In fact we are Siamese twins. Whatever happened for her in a healing session would also happen to me. We could feel each other's pain without knowing it, until we spoke on the phone. If I had something happening in my body that didn't make sense as soon as I spoke with her it became clear that it wasn't mine it was hers. It was only over time this all became clear to us. To help her with a session I wrote all this down as a diagram. The triangle and positive and negative were used a lot in my Psychosynthesis classes, so for some it will seem familiar.

SHIFTING ALL
THE TIME TO
ANOTHER *AND*
ANOTHER POSSIBILITY

POSSIBILITY
CHANGE
MOVING FORWARD
LETTING GO OF FEAR

**AND**

Generational
cultural beliefs

Generational
thought patterns

*all of these patterns feed a
positive and a negative side*

POSITIVE

NEGATIVE

| Maori & Celts (Irish/Scot) | | **WARS** | | Pakeha & English |
| Native American Indians | | **HATE** | | White American |
| People of Colour & Aboriginals | | **ATROCITIES** | | White American & White Australian |

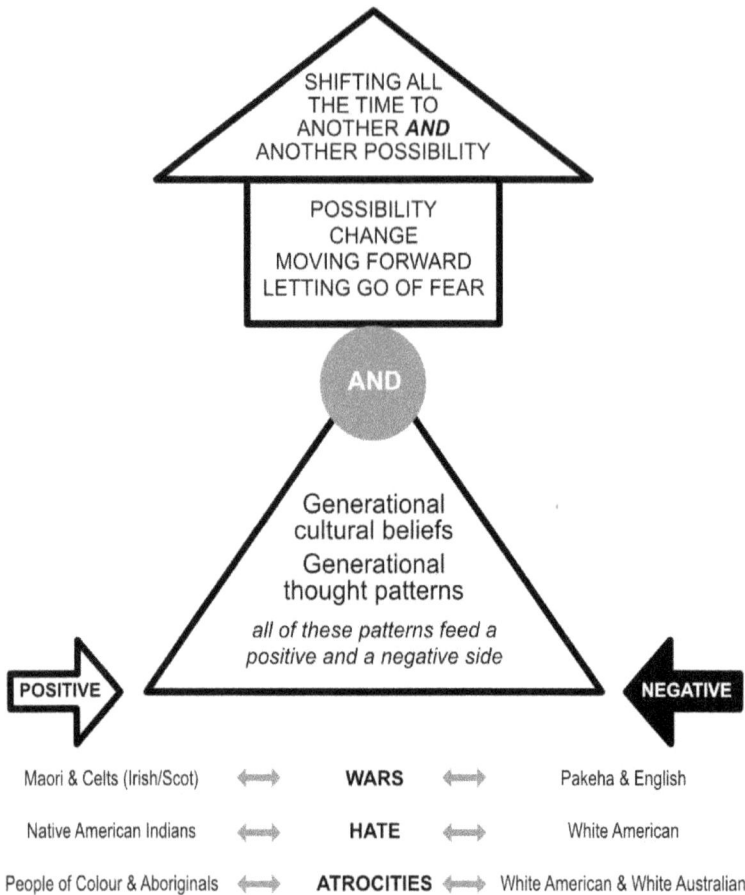

On the cultural side you have
blame, revenge, divide,
victim or activist with hate *not* love

On the white side you have
rule, conquer, sole supremacy

Different cultures, different countries, different ways of doing things and believing in
BUT THEY ULTIMATELY COME FROM FEAR **_NOT_** LOVE.
It is all done in the name of culture or religion

Culture can hold us back if it comes from fear
Religion can hold us back if it comes from fear

Different cultures, different countries, different ways of doing
Things and believing in
**BUT ULTIMATELY THEY COME FROM FEAR AND
CONTROL NOT LOVE.**
It is all done in the name of culture or religion
Culture can hold us back if it comes from fear
Religion can hold us back if it comes from fear

When you move away from either side of positive or negative you have the AND. There is no positive or negative, there is no side, it just IS. The AND, brings everything back into balance. You can have too much on a positive side and too much on the negative side. Either way there is no balance. If you do away with both and find the AND, you will find the solution to what has been, and find what can be

This is POSSIBILITY ....... This is possibility of growth, change and love and light

When we release anything comes from fear or hate, whether it is cultural or religious, then we are able to shift to a new paradigm where we move away from fear and we are able to move to love.

The land and I merge as one and become one. There are no claims for ownership of the land and to undo the wrongs of the past over land we must acknowledge the land belongs to everyone, not to one sole culture or race.

When this came up for me it helped me explain to her the importance of why she had to let go of generational beliefs. When you are embedded in a strong culture that says it is working and doing the best for you, yet in reality

173

all it is doing is killing you, it is time to change. We are all ultimately ruled by fear and the need to conquer. Ideas are based on the notion of weed out the weak and the strong shall survive. This approach keeps the legacy of hate and fear alive over the generations. Ever since time began it has been like this. We are now at a point in life that we need to look at this and change it.

When you do your inner work this is exactly what you doing, you are changing what you have been told to believe in. If it no longer sits well with you, you change it. This goes to what I have said throughout the book; if you stand and face your fear and it will dissipate and no longer have a hold over you. You will start to find what you believe in to no longer be true, so seek what you believe in and do not settle for what you have been told to believe in the name of culture or religion. You no longer come from fear; you come from love which will never let you down. Understand this love is not the love we have with husbands and wives. It is much bigger than that. This love is a love for self, humanity, the universe; pure unconditional love. So if we are to believe the saying from the beginning of this chapter, Love makes the world go round," to help that happen we need to first work on ourselves so love can truly overcome all.

## Chapter Fifteen
## Choose love or fear

*Bring our body, our mind and our spirit back into
balance
Then we will be in alignment with the Universe*

There are only two choices we have love or fear, that's
it. Once we can start to be aware of that then we can
make changes. Awareness is part of the key to opening
up and seeing properly for the first time. If we are not
aware then we go around blind all the time; although we
have eyes, we don't actually see. We can't change
anything if we are first not aware. I am often asking my
clients to become aware of what they are saying and how
their body feels. Our body is our guide. The only way it
can communicate with us is through pain. Some will take
notice and become aware of their body and stop and try
to fix it while others will choose to carry on and ignore
the body. Either way we need to be aware of what we
think how we think and what we feel. We need to be
aware of how we hold tension in the body and how are
we breathing. There are so many signals our body shows
us but we usually wait until we are at the last stage before
we get help. While the ambulance is at the top of the cliff
is when we should take action, not waiting until it's at the
bottom. We are all too busy. Time after time I have heard
people say, "I'm too busy," "it costs too much," "that
doesn't sound right for me," "that won't work," "I'm

fine, I'm not stressed." Over and over I will say if you don't take the time now, you won't have a body to help you do all the things you need to. There are so many different ways of healing that you need to find what is right for you, what feels right; you will know when you find it.

Most of our body is made up of it is muscle. They dominate the entire body and we can't do anything without using our muscles. When I was doing my Nurse Training we were never taught how important muscle was, apart from the obvious things like the muscle around the heart. When I started my massage training and began to learn about the importance of muscle I was really annoyed as I felt the information I had now could have helped me care for patients a bit differently. With more awareness around the body and muscles I could have paid a bit more attention and focus on it. Of course back then I doubt very much the medical profession would have been prepared to look at the body differently. Medicine isn't just about taking tablets to fix a problem; it's up to us to listen to what our body is telling us it wants us to do. I don't want to say alternative as I feel we should routinely look at our body this way instead of viewing it as alternative. I say this is about trying to prevent, not necessarily about cure. This of course may seem foreign to some but let's face it, who knows our body better than us, no one. So why do we think we need to hand the control over to others to look after our body's? Shouldn't that be our job?

After many years of doing inner work on myself I saw in a meditation that my body was so far behind as I had been concentrating on psychological issues and forgotten about my body. I had been concentrating on doing all the inner work and hadn't realised my body also needed work. My mind was coming along just fine, but my body was a different matter. It is our body that hold onto everything it feels, is told, we hold all our emotional rubbish in our body's. So it only makes sense that we get work done on our bodies as well. They work hand in hand, work on the psychological side but also on the body at the same time so that they can work together to release old stagnant energies, old fears, old hurts. If we are able to this then everything releases a lot quicker.

I talk about bringing everything back into balance. Our bodies are designed to heal themselves if we allow them to, but as mentioned; we are often too busy and want quick fixes or someone else to fix the problem. We do not take responsibility for ourselves. Taking responsibility for ourselves involves taking a good hard look at ourselves and seeing what we need to change. The mind, heart and body need to work together. Some say we don't need the mind, just the heart and body, but I personally don't think that is quite true. It has been our minds that have lead us to where we are now in our evolution after we cut ourselves away from our hearts and bodies. Our mind has been the dominant organ, yet we can't survive without heart or body. We have become so used to the mind being in charge that we have forgotten what it is like to feel our bodies and feel what is right for us. We think about it, we don't feel it. Now is the time to bring all three together. We need to not use the mind as much, not think too much but start to feel again. Start to be aware of how you feel, start to feel your body and get to know it so it is less of a stranger; my body is unique, I love my body and I love how I feel. I found a saying I have up in my toilet for everyone to read that says, **"Feelings are thoughts in motion in our**

**bodies. We can't heal what we can't feel, so we must feel our feelings**." Unfortunately I can't remember where I found it, but it's very appropriate I think.

Most of my clients don't breathe properly, so I make them aware of how they are breathing and how they can try and change it. At first they are consciously thinking about it, "I think this is what I am doing. I'm sure I'm breathing properly." I get them to feel how they are breathing by being aware of what they are doing. By feeling their body's change when they let out a big deep breath and can feel their shoulders drop or their bodies get heavier on the table, they are feeling how their bodies are. This is getting them out of their heads and into their body's. Everyone initially struggles doing this; even I did and still can at times. Most of the times we are breath shallow and never really expel the air out of our lungs, we just keep re-circulating old oxygen with new oxygen, never letting anything out. When we pay attention to how we are breathing and do it properly, it is amazing what the body can let go of, and how it makes us feel. Generally we will feel lighter, freer, not so heavy or dense and that's all just from breathing and letting everything out. Again, if we pay attention to how our body feels, it will show us what we are to do to help let go of what needs to be released.

Everything in life is about balance. No more so than our body and mind. To heal and let go we need to engage all three: body, mind and heart. It is now time for our hearts to take the lead and let the mind rest. We still use our minds though, for if it wasn't for the mind we wouldn't be here today. So we need to bring our hearts back into line with the mind, so they can work together in balance and in harmony, never to be separated again.

Our bodies are truly unique and they are the best guides we can ever have here in the physical world we live in. Remember though we are **"spiritual beings in a physical body"** so there is a lot more to our body than we have discovered. If we are open to it all, we will be shown, but we must listen and feel our bodies as well as doing our inner work! The world literally is our oyster if we allow it to be.

Going back to me being abused by my dad when I was younger, my mind may have kept the memory of it dormant for so long, my body, however, never forgot. That's the difference our minds can trick us and play games by telling us what we think we want to hear or know. Our bodies can never lie, never, that is why it is so important to pay attention to our bodies and get some work done on them. Many times I have clients tell me what they think I want to hear when I ask them how their body is. Yet when they lie on the table the body tells me something totally different, I always listen to what the body is telling me, not quite so much the clients in this instance.

# Conclusion

It's been four years since I started writing this book. It's had ups and downs as mentioned, but I have managed to get through them all. Never in my wildest dreams did I think it would have taken four years to finish. When I started I was motivated and ready to get on with writing, so I went full steam ahead with gusto. That is until I came to my hurdles and stopped! Not knowingly of course, it wasn't until I looked back at the chapters and realised why I had stopped. Everything happens in its own time, everything happens for a reason, and when writing I still had issues to deal with when they came up. I still had to release old stagnant energies that were stuck around the issues I had, which were mainly emotional of course. That's the beauty of this work; it never stops until you stop breathing. It is ongoing, but you get better at recognizing your issues and dealing with them. It no longer takes weeks or days to clear things; they can be gone in a few hours literally, and clearing becomes that quick as you get more proficient at it on all levels.

This journey of writing my story has been amazing, scary but also liberating at the same time. Knowing that if I can change one person lives by them deciding to change, then I have achieved what I set out to do. It wasn't just about the writing; this was part of my healing as well.

As I said right back at the beginning I am a private person, so writing my story was scary and yes I was fearful of what people would think, say and they would not believe me. I have been shown many, many a time if you do what you are shown it all works out well. In the end, how people will react to my story is their choice. I could let that fear of being judged stop me from writing but I haven't. Many years ago I would have done exactly that, let the fear win. Not today, I trust, follow and go inside and know all will be well.

So as I sit here today, coming to the end of writing this book, I am a changed person. I am changed from the individual who arrived upon these shores in 1997, and I am different from even the soul who started writing this back in 2012. We have no choice but to change as we learn and grow, as we let go of the old and make way for the new. I will keep changing, my views may change, as I learn more, but the fundamentals of what I have learnt will still be the same. It is up to us and only we can change ourselves, no one else can do it for us. I could have quite easily put myself down as a victim of sexual abuse, but I didn't. I feel it would have limited me to being able to change as I would have always had that label of victim. Yes it happened, yes I went through all the unimaginable emotions and self-doubt, disbelief, hurt, anger, blame that any person does when they discover this has happened to them. I didn't let it make me a victim to the circumstances though. If I had I wouldn't have allowed myself to look at it, acknowledge it, accept it and move on. It will always be there, that will never get taken away as I can't change what happened, but I can change how I look at it, what I do about it. If I make myself a victim of it I am holding on to all those horrible emotions, they are hurting me, no one else. Not the person who did it, not the other family members, but me, it's hurting me. I am damaging my spirit, my soul is being taken away from me, the longer I hold onto to the hurt, the more I am slowly dying inside. No one can see that, but I can certainly feel it and deep down I know it. So where's the justice in that, I am hurting myself as well as having been abused. It doesn't make sense does it, yet that's what we do.

It was through Psychosynthesis that showed me that. Jay talked about not becoming the victim and I have since heard it from others as well. Now I can see it makes sense, yet back then I really struggled with that concept at first. There was a part of me that did want to be the victim, but there was also a part that said no. Thankfully meeting these people has helped me achieve that shift. It would have been so easy to be stuck in victim if I hadn't been told there is another way of dealing with the atrocities that happen to us. It is possible to live life to the full, have trust in yourself and believe in yourself. We can learn and move forward from what has happened, or we stay stuck, never moving on with everything falling apart, around us.

It's not about getting to your destination quickly; it's about being on the journey, helping you arrive at your destination. It's all about the journey not the destination. It's all about forgiving and not holding grudges or resentments. It's all about being content where you are and with what you have; if you aren't then you need to take action to change things. It's all about following your own guidance, no one else's. It's all about coming from a place of love not fear. Take that leap of faith and jump, just do it, don't think about it, do it.

When I look back now, I can see everything happened for a reason. I was lead to these shores to take a good hard look at myself. I had started my healing when I started counselling back in Britain but I needed more, and coming to New Zealand has done that for me. Was it coincidence, no, I was following what I felt I needed to do; I was following my gut instinct. I just didn't see it like that. If I had been told you are off to New Zealand to do some really hard inner work on yourself, do you think I would have gone, of course not? I would have been too scared to, not wanting to do anything like that, so I would have run, and kept on running. Yet here I am being thankful for what I have done and will continue to do. I could have quite easily not followed my instinct and not come. Where would I be today? Still stuck in myself pity, poor me, still blaming others and still angry, I am guessing. That is where choice comes into it, we have freedom of choice, it is up to us, we can live by fear, or we can turn around face our fears and be liberated from them. I know what sounds better to me, what about you?

*We have eyes, yet don't see*
*We have ears, yet don't hear*
*We have mouths, yet don't speak*
*We have souls, yet are soul-less*
*We are spirit, yet are spirit-less*

*When we look inside us and believe, then we can see*
*When we look inside us and believe, then we can hear*
*When we look inside us and believe, then we can speak*
*When we look inside us and believe, then we are soul*
*When we look inside us and believe, then we are spirit*

*Turn around and face your fear*
*Do not be afraid*
*There is hope in believing and trusting*
*There are answers to many unanswered questions*
*The answer always lives inside of you*
*You have the key to your own salvation – no one else*

*Believe in you*
*Trust in you*
*Celebrate in you*
*Follow you*
*Love you*

It is with love and hope that some will be able to change what you do. For others that don't, hold onto the prospect that later on down the track when you are ready you can. For those who truly don't want to see or understand change, I offer you love and light.

To everyone who has picked up this book and read it I thank you. You were drawn to it and followed through reading it, I congratulate you. Now comes the time for you to make that change you know you need to, want to. Have faith in you and you can achieve, reach for those stars for they are yours for taking, and dare to dream. Find that star out there that is solely yours and it will guide you to your true self.

That's my story
What's yours?

# Post Script

Since writing this down I have been reading again, after being told to stop for a while. How I love that there is such a world of knowledge and information out there in books that were written many centuries ago. For me it was unknown, until now. Hence I feel so compelled to write about it. I have just re read over chapter one, proof reading before I publish and feel I need to add a bit more.

I read a book called the *Dead Sea Scrolls Deception* by Michael Baigent and Richard Leigh, it talks about the discovery of the scrolls and how the church virtually had full control of what information was released and who was given permission to access these, once the church had validated the information first, of course, so under control. It certainly makes for an interesting read, some I definitely get confused but can make sense out of most of the information. I was curious to see what other books the authors had co-written and so had a look. I was drawn to a book called The Elixir And The Stone and with modern technology and the help of my kindle I had the book instantly. Straight away I was hooked on the book, talking about magic, symbols and a lot more.

What really grabbed my attention, however, was a term that was used I had never heard of until then. That term was called "hermetic," being connected with nature. Basically what I took from reading this book is that all thoughts and walks of people, regardless of what they believed in, which God they worshipped they were all tolerant of each other and got along, imagine that! But, even more than that, throughout our entire history there has been a way of thinking that is conducive with living at harmony with nature, living in peace with all and respecting all. When you listen to some people who class themselves as new age and how they talk I assumed this was something new to our generation, blindly or not I don't know. This book showed me this is not the case and that way of believing and being is as old as time itself. There is nothing new in believing in yourself and following your instinct. There is nothing new in tolerating and getting along with all creeds of religions, thoughts and beliefs. There is also nothing new in the fact that authorities don't like that, as they have no control and so do everything in their power to change that, be it through war, inquisitions, and all the other atrocities' that have occurred throughout History. Here I was thinking this is all a new way of thinking as our generations evolve, yet that is anything from the truth, this way of being is ancient.

So many pioneer explorers wanting to spread the word of what life could be like, yet each of them taken down. However, a secret society was set up to combat this: the Rosicrucian Society. According to the authors it had many a famous member. For anyone wanting to know more or even curious I would highly recommend this book.

I was blown away with the realisation that nothing is new, all the information is there and had always been there for us to access, if we choose to. I watched a movie called *The Man who knew Infinity*; great movie. It also said "everything we need to know about the universe is there; we just need to access it." Now how can that information change our thinking and way of being?

# Appendix

## Meditation

One way to help us start to find our true self is by doing meditation. We move from our head space into our heart space. This is where we truly are.

Meditation can take on many different ways and forms; there is no right or wrong way. Just sit or lie and allow yourself to just be.

What I am about to write here is to help get you started, not too complicated and doesn't have to take up a lot of time (time is always one factor that puts people off from even trying, so I always say even two to three minutes is better than none) Do not worry about time, just allow yourself to try it.

This is your time, so value that; have no phone calls, no distractions, make sure you know you won't be interrupted, remember it will take as long as what you want it to.

Find a nice quiet spot to sit
Light a candle
When first starting you can have soft gentle music playing if you wish
Sit yourself comfortably
Breathe in and out a few times

Allow yourself to relax

Close our eyes and concentrate on your breathing. As you breathe in say "I am peace," as you breathe out say "I am light," each time you breathe just say those words or something else, so long as you are saying something that is positive, could be "I am love, I am light, I am peace, I am hope, I am joy," so long as it resonates with you it doesn't matter. At first it doesn't matter if you don't believe it, you are saying this to try and stop the chatter in your mind. Over time you won't only believe it but you will also feel it, amazing.

You are still going to have your mind "I can't do this," "this is too hard," "I have washing to put out, dishes to do" and so on; don't worry about that, just turn around and say, "I will deal with you when I have finished." With you doing this you are acknowledging your mind, but telling it not right now, I will deal with you soon. This is huge, and please do try it. If you try and ignore it by falling into the trap of thinking "I'm meditating so not allowed to have thoughts, go away," you will find you will only get more frustrated, the thoughts will get bigger and more demanding until eventually you have had enough and will give up, thinking you can't meditate waste of time. NOT SO, acknowledge your thoughts but don't let them take over as they usually do. This is you starting to change and take control back. You CAN do it; more importantly, you MUST do it.

All this takes is a few minutes, it doesn't matter how long, what does matter is that you start and continue. Over time you will stay longer, it all depends on where you are at on the day, that's all.

If you still find even doing this task hard, try just staring at the flame of the candle, breathing in and out. This way you are taking a few moments out, then you might find your eyes will close and just breathe in and out, just sit and be peaceful with it.

This is a very basic form of meditation to get you started. There are many different ways; you just need to find which way you like. That can be either from reading a book, attending a class, having a CD, or listening to music, it doesn't matter, so long as you try and do it.

## Breathing

This is breathing to relax and let go of tension and held onto emotions:

Again sit in a quiet place, take a few moments. Start by breathing in through your nose, with your mouth closed. As you breathe in have your hands down on your tummy, so you can feel your diaphragm rise up. As you breathe out, open your mouth nice and wide and let all the air out. As you repeat this a few times, you will start to feel your shoulders drop; you will feel heavier where ever you are sitting; now you are allowing your body and yourself to relax. You are starting to connect with your body through your breathing.

If you find yourself getting wound up or annoyed, frustrated throughout the day, take a step back from where you are standing, and take a few breaths as described above, notice if you feel any different, you should. If for whatever reason you don't, keep doing the breathing until you can feel something has shifted.

When you are in bed, another great way of breathing is by starting from your toes and feet; you are going to breathe into them, see how your feet and toes feel, where there is tension, then you will breathe in and out into them allowing the tension to go. You will work up to your legs, knees, thighs, buttocks, abdomen, back, chest, arms, hands, shoulders, neck, throat, face, eyes, lips, ears, mouth, nose, head. You breathe into every part of your body and as you breathe out you are allowing the tension to leave that part of your body. Again this is a way to help you connect back in with your body. Many yoga instructors will do this type of exercise at the end of their sessions.

These are two very simple yet effective ways of helping to get you started. Like the meditation section you will find other ways of doing as well, you just need to start and see what feels right for your body.

Do not be fooled by the mind saying, "this is rubbish I can't do this, it's not working." No it isn't and yes it is working; it will take a little while for you to feel that. Remember the mind has been in control for so long, it doesn't want to hand over the reins so easy, but through practise and perseverance on your part that will change, it still comes down to you, and only you. Have trust, you can do it.

**Please remember these are just some brief descriptions to help get you started. However, all of us need to get professional help at some stage. If things are getting on top of you, if you are not dealing with life, if anything has resonated with you in this book, then you would benefit from professional help. I have listed below some books**

and two sites, but there are a lot more out there. I always say to people, when you start looking whoever jumps out at you they are the ones for you to see. Talk, write, meditate, breathe, and get help.

# Bibliography

Baignet, Michael, and Richard Leigh. *The Dead Sea Scroll Deception*. (Random House, 1991)

Baignet, Michael, and Richard Leigh. *The Elixir and the Stone*. (Arrow Books, 2013)

Brown, Dan. *The Da Vinci Code*. (Doubleday, 2003)

Burnstein, Dan. *Secret of the Code: The unauthorised guide to the mysteries behind the Da Vinci Code*. (Weidenfeld & Nicolson, 2004)

Crossingham, Lesley. *Amma'Na Tha, The forgotten wisdom of Mary Magdalene*. ( Shannon Books, 2006)

Lipton, Bruce, and Steve Bhaerman. *Spontaneous Evolution, our positive future (and a way to get there from here)*. (Hayhouse Inc, 2009)

Nicholson, Sue. *A call from the other side*. (Wellington, 2007)

Tolle, Eckhart. *The Power of Now.* (Hodder, 2004)

# Resources

www.natural therapy pages.co.nz

www.psychosynthesis

# List of some authors

Alice Bailey

Barry Braislford

Bruce Lipton

Caroline Myss

Colin Fry

Dali Lama

Dawson Church

Donna Eden

Doreen Virtue

Eckhart Tolle

H.P. Blavatsky

James Redfield

John O'Donohue

Julia Cameron

Kelvin Cruickshank

Lesley Crossingham

Lucy Cavendish

Master Choa kok sui

Michael Baigent

Michael Roads

Michael Sheridan

Neale Walsh

Richard Leigh

Richard Moss

Roberto Assagioli

Rosemary Altea

Sparrowhawk (Jay Ray)

Sue Nicholson

Susun Weed

Sylvia Browne

Wayne Dwyer

www.ingramcontent.com/pod-product-compliance
Lightning Source LLC
Chambersburg PA
CBHW051825040426

42447CB00006B/366